GW01417562

Northern England
Edited by Chris Hallam

Young**Writers**

First published in Great Britain in 2004 by:
Young Writers
Remus House
Coltsfoot Drive
Peterborough
PE2 9JX
Telephone: 01733 890066
Website: www.youngwriters.co.uk

SB ISBN 1 84460 374 1

Foreword

This year, the Young Writers' 'Poetry In Motion' competition proudly presents a showcase of the best poetic talent selected from over 40,000 up-and-coming writers nationwide.

Young Writers was established in 1991 to promote the reading and writing of poetry within schools and to the youth of today. Our books nurture and inspire confidence in the ability of young writers and provide a snapshot of poems written in schools and at home by budding poets of the future.

The thought effort, imagination and hard work put into each poem impressed us all and the task of selecting poems was a difficult but nevertheless enjoyable experience.

We hope you are as pleased as we are with the final selection and that you and your family continue to be entertained with *Poetry In Motion Northern England* for many years to come.

Contents

Billingham Campus School, Billingham

Lisa Wilson (13)   21
Sammie-Jo Clayton (11)   21
Nikki Young (13)   22
Rebecca Higgins (14)   22
Anna Leigh Turnbull (13)   23
Natalie Sigsworth (14)   23
Gemma Bedlington (11)   24

Burnside Community High School, Wallsend
Sarah Lee (15)   25

Catcote School, Hartlepool
Michael Warren (15)   26
Ashley Aston (13)   26
Marc Hodge (14)   27
Alan Juillerat (14)   27
Robert Pounder (18)   28
Jane Ducker (14)   28

Central Newcastle High School, Newcastle-Upon-Tyne
Laura Bland (11)   29
Christine Clark (11)   30
Georgina Davison (12)   30
Emily Cogan (11)   31
Elspeth Crawford (11)   31
Laura Cuthbertson (12)   32
Holly Elsdon (11)   32
Megan Shaw (11)   33
Emma Florek (11)   34
Polly Marlow (11)   35
Amy Harrison (12)   36
Rebecca Jameson (11)   37
Rose Hodgson (11)   38
Anupriya Singh (12)   38
Amaani Hussain (11)   39
Sophie R Robertson (11)   39
Jane Stockdale (11)   40
Sophie Winter (11)   40
Chantal Yeung (12)   41

Dyke House School, Hartlepool

Laura Calvert (13)	41
Adam Hinks (13)	42
Anthony Heron (13)	42
Matthew Price (13)	43
Emma Calvert (13)	43
Kimberley White (13)	44
Chris Charlton (13)	44
Gemma Sharpe (13)	45
Jade Ainsley (13)	46
Craig Lythe (14)	46
Emma Swainson (13)	47
Steven Smurthwaite (13)	47
Shaun Foxon (13)	48
Matthew Forcer (13)	48
Daniel Begley (14)	49
Nicola Robinson (13)	49
Shannon Davis (13)	50
Jonathan Hill (14)	50
Kathryn Hall (13)	50
Leanne Whitelock (13)	51

Eston Park School, Middlesbrough

Xhul Islami (12)	52
Rachel Gregory (12)	52
John Thrower (12)	53
Carl Wilson (12)	53
James Eades (12)	54
Abi Winton-Wright (12)	54
Kelly Stephenson (12)	55
Ashleigh Hannah (12)	55
Samantha Stephenson (12)	56
Lewis Rawles (12)	57
Sam Sanderson (13)	58
Emily McPartland (12)	58
Gemma Havelock (13)	59
Lee Keenan (12)	59
Liane McGovern (13)	60
Tanya Davison (12)	61
Rosie Stockil (12)	62
Emma Todd (12)	62

Nicola Jones (12)   63
Michael Cockerill (12)   63
Fenella Charles (12)   64
Jessica Harrison (12)   65
Lucy Yeomans (12)   66
Helen Gavillet (12)   67
Lauren Doddy (12)   68
Joanne Taylor (12)   68
Josh Groves (12)   69
Rachel Rowland (12)   69
Dean Evans (12)   70
Hayley Byrne (13)   70
Beth Cochran (12)   71
Michael Kirkham (12)   72
Stacey Wright (12)   73
Nicola Jones (12)   74
Rebecca McAllister (12)   75
Paul Keenan (12)   76

George Stephenson High School, Tyne & Wear
Trisha Purvis (15)   76
Claire Scott (12)   77
Jasmin McKenzie (11)   78
Charlotte Harrison (12)   78
Chelsea Kingston (12)   79
Ashleigh Lyon (12)   80

King Edward VI High School, Morpeth
Kylie Wood (15)   80
Emma Hodgkinson (15)   81

Macmillan College, Middlesbrough
Katie Thomas (14)   82
Bethany Longstaff (14)   83
Emma Carr (13)   84

Mardon Bridge Middle School, Whitley Bay
Matthew Vaughan (12)   85
Sophie Horsborough (12)   85
Chelsea Howson (12)   86

Danielle Fox (12)	86
Georgia Whinfield (12)	87
Nicole Reid (12)	87
Tom Smith (12)	88
Callum Callighan (12)	88
Yasmin Begum (12)	89
Jessica Wragg (12)	89
Laura Wilson (12)	90
Daniel Kingswood (12)	90
Charlotte O'Neil (12)	91
Daniel Crow (12)	91
Adam Sloan (12)	92
Anna Stevens (12)	92
Christopher Swan (12)	93
Craig Lydall (12)	93
Marni Mather (12)	94
Thomas Flynn (12)	94
Amy Forbes (12)	95
Laura Wall (12)	95
Marie Husthwaite (12)	96
Lauren Tudor (12)	96
Phoebe Friggens (12)	97
Gina Wade (12)	97
Matthew Wilson (12)	98
Shiuli Rahman (12)	98
Aimee Downey (12)	99
Mark Errington (12)	99
Sam Erskine (12)	100
Emma Roberts (12)	100
Stephanie Legg (12)	101
Richard Newton (13)	101
Sam Tack (12)	102
Lawrence Rainbow (12)	102
Ruth Tonks (12)	103
Liam McEwan (12)	103
Taylor-Jay Hyde (12)	104
Patrick Owers (12)	104
Siobhan Kemp (12)	105
James Auchterlonie (12)	105
Thomas Perry (12)	106
Emma Dillon (12)	106
Beth Newman (13)	107

Ormesby Comprehensive School, Middlesbrough

Drew Moore (12)	129
Sara Mawson (13)	130
Yolanda Hughes (13)	131
Samantha Collins (12)	132
Tafadzwa Kuwaza (13)	133
Kate Whitehead (12)	134
Michael Maloney (12)	134
Samantha Pryde (13)	135
Aaron Boggett (13)	135
Kelly Broad (12)	136
James Blagg (12)	137
Tamsin Hugill (12)	138
Lewis Harvey (13)	138
Carl Thompson (12)	139
Shirley Halliday (12)	139
Liam Johnstone (12)	140
Dean Harper (13)	141
Christopher Rose (12)	142
Christopher Metcalfe (12)	142
Jamie Williams (12)	143
Nicki Adams (12)	143
Ashleigh Blake (13)	144
Matthew Carter (12)	144
Lisa Baker (12)	145
Robert Keenan (12)	145
Philip Wilson (12)	146
Andrew McGarva (12)	146
Danny Wootton (12)	147
Katie Jacobs (12)	148
Darrell Finley (12)	149
Ashleigh Melton (12)	150
Adam Blowers (12)	151
Paul Readman (12)	152

St Edmund Campion RC School, Gateshead

Phillip McGill (11)	152
Lucy Harding (11)	153
Danielle Highton (11)	153
Sean Jackson (11)	154
Joanna Harding (12)	155

Rachael Harding (11) 156
Lee Gibson (11) 156
Kenneth Henderson (12) 157
Dean Birkbeck (11) 157
Cassandra Cameron (11) 158
Callum Whinham (11) 158
Antonia Armstrong (11) 159
Ashley Puntin (11) 160
Emma Conwell (12) 161
Rhoda Chambers (11) 162
Stephen Scott (11) 163
Adam Phillips (11) 164
Samantha Marley (11) 164
Karl Burns (11) 165
Michael Howard (11) 165
Emily Harrison (11) 166
Michael Gourley (11) 166
Kirsty Parker (11) 167
Samantha Walton (11) 167
Frances Saint (11) 168

West Redcar School, Redcar
Olivia McCann (13) 169
Emma O'Rourke (14) 169
Michael Delaney (13) 170
Stacy Young (13) 170
Sarah Turner (13) 171
Elizabeth Smith (14) 171
Carly Leigh Nolan (13) 172
Nathan Scrafton (13) 172
Kerry Melville (13) 173
Lucy Would (13) 173
Jamie Lewis (13) 174
Samantha Knight (13) 174
Emma Readman (13) 175
Kirsty Bass (13) 175

The Poems

Autumn And Winter

Autumn
Autumn leaves fall from the trees,
Under the sunlight sky,
Trees shiver from the cold wind,
Many people collect conkers,
Nevertheless people would rather
Stay at home.

Winter
Woolly hats and scarves
Ice covers the black roads,
No one is out, everything is silent,
The snow falls and covers roads and houses,
Everyone is happy at Christmas time,
Rivers freeze over.

Lauren McKenzie (12)
Billingham Campus School, Billingham

The House

The house was old and grey,
Even on a summer's day,
The door was rusty,
The stairs were dusty.

The second floor was ready,
The curtains were all dressy,
Cobwebs on the windowpane,
In the corner was a cane.

The man who lived there loved his chair,
He loved it without a care,
But when we looked through the window,
There was no one there.

Gemma Hotson (12)
Billingham Campus School, Billingham

Sadness

When I was about 3 years old,
My mam was ill,
I felt so sad and also so cold,
As I slowly walked into the room
Where my mam lay,
My heart began to thump,
My mam's green eyes started to close,
This was not a very good sign,
My dad told me that everything was fine,
But I knew that it wasn't.

I began to cry,
I hated to think that my mam was hurt and ill,
But that was what was true,
I had to get used to it and from that day on,
My mam was ill and two years after that day, she died,
I was hurt, hurt as anyone could ever be.

Samantha Owens (11)
Billingham Campus School, Billingham

Winter And Summer

I love the winter every year,
I have to wear lots of fur,
Catching snowflakes on our tongue,
Little ripples, water runs.

I hate the summer hot and sweaty,
I always cuddle my teddy Betty,
I always have to drink,
I am always drawing with lots of ink.

Jade Love (11)
Billingham Campus School, Billingham

Past Times

As I sit up in my room,
I listen to my heart go boom.
My mind recalls my dreaded past
And why our love didn't last.

I think about why you left
And all those things I should have said.
In the back of my mind I hear the screams,
The shrieks in the night, the water of streams.

I remember the walk down by the rocks,
The sounds in my head of metal locks.
The clank of a pea that lies in my skull,
The thought that's inside a fuming bull.

With eyes like fire, a pounding beat,
The fear inside, I need to eat.
In the end it all calms down,
As I feel my body hit the ground.

That is the end, now can't you see,
There's nothing left inside of me.
So you must leave, and I must go
This is the past of my ego.

Katy Shrimpton (14)
Billingham Campus School, Billingham

Ghosts

One night I lay in my bed, scared,
I lay under my quilt, scared,
Waiting for a monster, scared,
Want to turn my light on, scared,
Peeping out my quilt, scared,
Lying back on my pillow, scared,
I'm really scared now!
Zzzzzzz.

Anthony Griffiths (11)
Billingham Campus School, Billingham

Weather

> Weather is hot
> Weather is cold
> Weather is wet
> Weather is snow.

Hot and sticky smells all through summer,
Wasps and bees following our ice creams,
When the winter comes it's even more fun,
It is so cold when the snow comes.

> Weather is hot
> Weather is cold
> Weather is wet
> Weather is snow.

So wherever we go weather will always be there,
Blowing or shining down on our hair,
All through autumn the leaves blowing around
And conkers are falling to the ground.

> Weather is hot
> Weather is cold
> Weather is wet
> Weather is snow.

Lisa Enderwick (12)
Billingham Campus School, Billingham

The Spooky House

Everyone says on a full moon the house on top of Morgan Hill
Has ghosts go there and celebrate,
You can't sleep because of the noise,
It shocks you, it deafens you.
A group of them usually swoop down
And sprinkle nightmare dust over you,
When you wake up, all you can see is darkness and fire.

Jordan Wright (11)
Billingham Campus School, Billingham

The Day That I Die

The house I've lived in for 13 years
And my bedroom decorated in tiger furs,
The field I've spent happy times
And the beck filled with rubbish and grime.

Leaving my friends
And their trends,
Leaving my hobbies
And my dog Dobby.

I'm going somewhere I've never seen,
I'm going somewhere no one here's been,
I'm going where the angels soar high,
Yes, you've got it, I'm going to die.

Leaving my friends
And their trends,
Leaving my hobbies
And my dog Dobby.

This is the end of my line,
Cancer's my star sign,
Cancer I've got
I'm here dying in my cot!

Pippa Shepherd (13)
Billingham Campus School, Billingham

Noises

Noises from the wind hitting my window,
Noises when cars pass by,
Noises come from Dad when he is snoring,
Noises when my mum's angry,
Noises when my sister cries,
Noises everywhere.

Ben Kelly (11)
Billingham Campus School, Billingham

Leaving, Leaving, Left

For many a week,
I have planned what I seek,
The pressure has reached its summit,
I'm leaving.

You do not care,
That my heart is so bare,
I hope your fresh lives plummet,
I'm leaving.

I creep down a stair,
Leaving you unaware,
I'm going for good right now,
I'm leaving.

You would want me to stay,
To say bye in a way,
But I would not know how,
I'm leaving, I'm leaving, I've left.

Calum Bambro (13)
Billingham Campus School, Billingham

The Darkness In The Alley

One dark, stormy night,
I was walking down an alley,
I bumped into this boy,
I knew who he was,
I didn't dare say it,
He said, 'Hello,' then walked off,
We both shouted, 'Bye,'
Then the next day we saw each other,
And didn't speak.

Chantelle Cuthbert (11)
Billingham Campus School, Billingham

Leaving

Sixteen, fifteen, fourteen, thirteen,
This is how I feel,
Upset and depressed that's what I am,
I like this place, it's them who spoil it.

Twelve, eleven, ten, nine,
My time here is getting shorter,
I don't feel like doing it,
I feel I have hurried through my life,
I'm going deeper underground as each day passes.

Eight, seven, six, five,
I am really weak but ready now,
I pack my bag ready for the right time to go,
It's time now, let's go!
I grab my bag, I grab my coat and out the door I go.

Four, three, two, one,
My time is up,
I have gone,
No one will ever see me again,
So this is my final goodbye,
I will miss you.

Ashleigh Gardner (13)
Billingham Campus School, Billingham

My Day In Space

My day in space was full of grace,
It was hard to put on a face,
As I floated through the air,
I had given space a brand new flair,
With me laughing, giggling in mid-air,
Gazing at the lonely stars,
With Jupiter, Neptune and Mars.

Daniel Hollingsworth (12)
Billingham Campus School, Billingham

Ice Cream

I was playing with my mate,
It was about half-past eight,
Then went the tune,
I ran out of my room,
To get to the ice cream van.

Swirling and whirling it went into the cone,
My ice cream was getting made,
It only took 5 minutes but
It felt like it took 5 days.

I asked for all the sauces,
Strawberry, chocolate and lime,
My mouth began to water
And my mouth began to whine.

He passed me my ice cream,
The one I had waited for,
I started to run home with it,
Then it fell from the cone to the floor.

Jodi-Lea Simpson (13)
Billingham Campus School, Billingham

Super Dad

My dad is like a super dad
Because he goes out all day,
Helping people, then he comes
Home and he looks after
Two little monsters, he cooks their food,
My dad loves helping whenever he can,
Even when he's poorly, he still goes on,
He's too busy helping us and
Everyone else,
That's my dad!

Hannah Willmott (12)
Billingham Campus School, Billingham

Away From Home!

As she leaves home after so many years,
She leaves a note at the top of the stairs,
Inside the note, it explains how she feels,
She knows her parents will be saying,
'Don't go, please.'
But she has to get away from there,
She has to get her parents out of her hair,
She looks at the note as she goes down the stairs,
She looks at her parents and sends them her prayers,
As she leaves through the front door, she is feeling regret,
She says in her mind to her parents,
Please don't fret!
There on the path stands her dream man,
Waiting there in his blue van,
She jumps in and they soon ride away,
Her parents will be saying,
'I wish we could have had one more day,'
She knows she's done wrong, but she knows she's done right,
Goodnight family, sleep tight!

Stefanie Hurren (13)
Billingham Campus School, Billingham

Trees!

Trees are big,
Trees are old,
Trees gather moss and mould,
Trees can grow anywhere
But not in water or up in the air,
Trees are planted in the ground,
Trees are wonkey,
Trees are round,
Trees, trees, they're everywhere,
All they do is stand and stare.

Joe Ivory (12)
Billingham Campus School, Billingham

Leaving

I have already told you I'm leaving,
You didn't listen before,
But now I've packed my stuff,
I'm walking out the door.

Please don't come after me,
I'm happier with my dad
And now that I am with him,
I know that I'll be glad.

I know that you still love me,
But things are not the same,
My life has changed so much,
You think that I'm a pain.

I hope you don't mind,
I really have to go,
I hope you understand,
But I'll love you even so.

Keisha Wood (13)
Billingham Campus School, Billingham

Witches' Spell

Lizard's leg and blind worm sting,
Cow's snout and a rolling pin,
Mix it up and it makes a broth.

Duck's foot and lad's hair,
A lost key and a rotten pear,
Mix it up and it makes a broth.

Rat's eye and a wolf's hand,
Insect's wing and a pop band,
Mix them up and it makes a broth.

Tracey McCallum (12)
Billingham Campus School, Billingham

Leaving

I'm sorry to say this
But what I am saying is true
You may think I don't love you
Believe me I do
I can hear him calling
And it's him who I choose
You don't care about me
When I ask for help, you just refuse.

I'm always upset
Can't live here anymore
I've been sick with the thought
And my heart, it is sore
Since Mum left us
You don't seem to care
Time is all around
Yet you still have none to spare
I'll love and remember you
Forever and more!
Goodbye.

Rachael Kisby (14)
Billingham Campus School, Billingham

Night-Time

Shiny stars in the sky,
I'm watching as the birds fly by,
The moon is glistening in my face,
As I lie in this unusual place.

Banging, crashing all around,
I'm wondering what is that sound?
It was once peace and quiet,
Now suddenly there is a riot.

Sophie McGreal (13)
Billingham Campus School, Billingham

My True Love

I ran away from love
Because it tore my heart apart
And now I've come back
To try a new start.

I've given it some time,
To let my heart heal
And now I'm in love
But this time it's for real.

He waited for me forever,
Just so he could be,
The sweetest lad I could ever see
And he means the world to me.

This gorgeous boy I feel
But could it just be fate,
Because I have finally found my love,
My best friend, my soulmate.

In the matter of just one day,
He puts a million smiles upon my face,
He can make me laugh forever,
No matter the time, nor place.

He's the only one, who knows exactly how I feel
And the words I need to say to him,
He's always there for me when I need someone the most,
In an understanding kinda way.

He treats me perfectly,
Every single day
And our love for one another,
Will always stay this way.

Katie Clayton (14)
Billingham Campus School, Billingham

Leaving

I'm leaving home, I'm leaving and everybody's screaming,
I'm leaving home, I'm leaving and everybody's grieving.

Going through a rough patch,
Going to leave the match,
Going to get lost,
Going to get covered in compost.

I'm leaving home, I'm leaving and everybody's screaming,
I'm leaving home, I'm leaving and everybody's grieving.

Going through the door,
Going to be a bore,
Leaving while they're mad,
Leaving while I'm sad.

I'm leaving home, I'm leaving and everybody's screaming,
I'm leaving home, I'm leaving and everybody's grieving.

Going down the street,
With nothing but a sheet,
Gone down the road,
Stepped on a toad.

I'm leaving home, I'm leaving and everybody's screaming,
I'm leaving home, I'm leaving and everybody's grieving.

Got hit by a car,
I'm splattered on the tar,
I'm leaving on a stretcher,
I'm going to meet Uncle Fletcher.

Michael Clegg (13)
Billingham Campus School, Billingham

Dying In The Dark

For the past nine months, I have planned
For this moment,
Nine minutes to end a nine month torment,
You have been told,
That your heart is so cold
And about me, you do not care.

I have left my miserable life
And ended it all with a knife,
I've slit my throat
And bleed on my coat,
But Mummy, I'm truly sorry.

Please tell sis to be brave
And tell big bro to behave,
Give Nanna my love
And Grandad a hug
And tell everyone, not to cry.

So now I say goodbye,
As I slowly die
And I will miss,
As I lie in bliss,
What little affection you gave.

Ben Armitage (13)
Billingham Campus School, Billingham

Heaven Above!

As the rain trickles down
Just like my tear
The heavens open
Awaiting for me
To take me up and look after thee.

Charlotte Sanderson (13)
Billingham Campus School, Billingham

Leaving!

I'm leaving home
It's time to go
But don't worry
I love you so.

Please don't be mad
Please don't be sad
Please just be glad
I'm moving in with Dad.

I'll see you soon
Don't move out
It will be OK
I'll be about.

Please don't be mad
Please don't be sad
Please just be glad
I'm moving in with Dad.

I'm not changing my mind
But I'll love you always
Please come and visit
I'll have open arms in the doorway.

Stephanie Waite (13)
Billingham Campus School, Billingham

Suicide

Lying here waiting to die,
As the sun sets in the sky,
As I watch the stars appear
I watch my life disappear.

It all goes dark and freezing cold,
As the sirens come up close,
Lying here in a hospital bed,
Rotting away because I'm dead!

Ben Lambotte (13)
Billingham Campus School, Billingham

The Tooth Fairy

Yesterday, my tooth fell out,
When I was on the roundabout,
Mum said don't look so glum
Because tonight the tooth fairy will come.

I couldn't wait to go to bed
Because of what my mum had said
My brother said she was a fake
Mum replied, 'For goodness sake!'

I went to bed at half-past eight,
Hoping the fairy wouldn't be late
I then began to count sheep,
Until I eventually fell asleep.

Next morning under my pillow
Guess what I found?
A golden coin shining and round,
I'm going to hide my money away,
Because my other nineteen teeth
Will fall out some day.

Elizabeth Jackson (12)
Billingham Campus School, Billingham

Spring

Hear the waterfall,
Thundering to the surface,
Like a blue diamond,
Hear the river flow,
Silently it passes you,
Come with me and hear,
Trees start to blossom,
Pretty colours appear,
The spring has started.

Andrew Cessford (13)
Billingham Campus School, Billingham

Leaving Home

I've told you that I'm leaving,
I've thought of this before,
I've lived my life unhappy,
I can't handle it anymore.

When I thought of walking out,
I promised that I'd stay,
Now I think it's time to go,
I'll soon be on my way.

I don't know where I'm going,
My mind spins round and round,
I'll move away to somewhere new,
My new life will soon be found.

Now I finally say goodbye,
Goodbye to all of you,
My life was dull and empty
And I made your life hell too.

Lauren Sigsworth (13)
Billingham Campus School, Billingham

Chocolate

Chocolate, dark, creamy, light,
Can't resist with all your might.

Twix, Maltesers and Dairy Milk,
Melts in your mouth and feels like silk.

Brown and sweet, it's like you're in Heaven,
But you'll be sick if you reach bar seven.

Chocolate is the best treat ever,
We'll buy a chocolate bar and eat it together.

Kimberley Boagey (13)
Billingham Campus School, Billingham

Dogs

Dogs are small and big
And like to dig,
They love dog food
In their bowl or in a dish,
That would be a wish,
They love to play
And run away,
Dogs care,
They are there,
They love you,
So what do you do?
Love them too?
Dogs hate cats,
But love their mats,
Dogs are there for you,
They are smart
And always bark,
But dogs like to play.

Rachel Grange (11)
Billingham Campus School, Billingham

Family Poem

Nana Pat isn't very fat,
Uncle Paul licks the wall,
Nana Mabel sits under the table,
Our sonny is so funny,
Aunty Leah likes her beer,
Aunty Jackie is from Falaraki,
Grandad Peter is a big eater,
Our Carl is a darl',
Our Jade likes lemonade
And my mam likes her man.

Natasha Durkin (13)
Billingham Campus School, Billingham

I Wish I Was Back There!

There was once a house,
It was filled with warmth and happiness,
Inside was a family of three,
So calm and lovely,
This house for them was a dream come true,
One day though, the two adults decided
Let's move away from here,
Thinking nobody minded,
The little girl who lived there
Though knew she would miss it so,
A few days passed and no one came to buy,
The house they shall foreclaim,
The little girl thought they were in with no luck,
Weeks passed and people came,
The family of three soon packed their bags again,
They have another house to go to,
The little girl started to cry,
For this was their last goodbye.

Sarah Shaw (13)
Billingham Campus School, Billingham

Bye

Now I am finally leaving home,
There is no time to moan,
I had to go straight away,
To live in Florida, Tampa Bay,
You disappeared on the relationship,
I was giving you too much lip,
I'm happy for what you did for me,
I hope you will still go to sea,
I'm going away forever,
To live with my boyfriend Trevor,
Bye.

Thomas Hunter (13)
Billingham Campus School, Billingham

She Is Leaving

She is crying now, she shall cry later,
Hiding her face from the bustling crowds,
Each in their own little worlds.

She is different from them,
She is leaving to meet another person in the forest,
Awaiting, waiting for someone who won't turn up.

She gave it up for him,
She gave it all for him,
She would have traded the world for him,
But heartbroken she walks away,
Crying now, crying later.

Joe Grange (13)
Billingham Campus School, Billingham

Leaving

I'm leaving home,
I have to go,
Should I forgive you?
I don't know.

I thought you cared,
You act like I'm dead,
You said you loved me,
'I never lie,' you said.

I've got to go,
I've started to pack,
So goodbye forever,
Cos I'm not coming back.

Lauren Watson (13)
Billingham Campus School, Billingham

I'm Gone For Good

I'm leaving now,
Don't try and find me,
You won't know how
Just relax, have a cup of tea.

I really do care,
But I have to leave,
I've taken my bear,
I need space to breathe.

Now I've gone,
You might be glad,
Or just maybe,
You will be sad.

I miss you all,
But it's for the best,
So trust me,
It's not just a test.

Lisa Wilson (13)
Billingham Campus School, Billingham

Only If The Sun

Only if the sun was there at night
And the moon was there at day
Then I'd run towards the sea
And let the sun shine down on me

Only if the sun looked at me in the night
Instead of the stars I think everyone
Would prefer the sun instead of the rain.

Sammie-Jo Clayton (11)
Billingham Campus School, Billingham

Time To Go

I have gone
Because you're a con,
Don't dis me
Or miss me,
By the way,
Your hair's like hay,
So is your mam's,
It smells like stale jam,
I've knicked your purse,
You'll need a nurse,
I have to go,
It's starting to snow,
See you later,
Alligator,
Time to go,
My fellow foe.

Nikki Young (13)
Billingham Campus School, Billingham

Dad

Dad I miss you so very much,
Your laugh, your smile, your loving touch,
We laughed and joked and talked a lot,
These memories will never be forgot.
It seems so hard to smile today,
Cos you're not here, you're far away,
A million tears I must have cried,
But I'll be strong cos you're by my side.
At times it seems we're so far apart,
But that's not true cos you live in my heart.

Rebecca Higgins (14)
Billingham Campus School, Billingham

Rain, Rain Come And Play

Rain, rain
Go away
It isn't time to come and play

So go back home you little thing
It's time to raid the cookie tin
Beside the cookie tin would lie
A lot of crumbs upon the sides
So up I climb to look right in
But there's no cookies in the tin.

So back outside I will stay
And tell the rain to come and play.
We would play upon the lawn
And wait until the morning's dawn.

Anna Leigh Turnbull (13)
Billingham Campus School, Billingham

Jane

I don't know who to talk to
I've never felt this bad
I'm stressed and angry constantly
I know I make you mad

I really need to get away
But don't know where to go
Would it be easier if I went
And left you all alone?

I went over to the kitchen drawer
And pulled out a large knife
Can you guess what happened next?
I took my young, sweet life.

Natalie Sigsworth (14)
Billingham Campus School, Billingham

Misty, Murky Morning

One misty, murky morning
I soon awoke in fright
To find someone lurking
Lurking out of sight

The wind was blowing
Furiously I ran right downstairs
I cuddled with my teddy bear
Shivering and scared

The wind was getting louder
Hissing in the air
I got a funny feeling
That someone was there

Shadows were moving in
Searching for food I
Tightened my arms and
Didn't even move

I heard a loud bang
And all the shadows left
I felt relieved and happy
It's over now, all over.

Gemma Bedlington (11)
Billingham Campus School, Billingham

Something's Changing

In the darkness something's changing
The heat leaves, the cold returns
The fire's gone out, the ice reforms
The sun has fallen there will be no dawn

The violent purple clouds of doom roll up
Electricity shrieks and leaps, flying through the air
The great war gods are angered
Their fury flies through a man's heart

The storm laughs as it tears at the sky
And the stones of the towers tremble
Hark all ye people apocalypse is nigh
I watch in fear as fire rains from on high

Will any be saved or will all perish?
My mind is chaotically calm in calamity
There is peace in the wars of gods
But war for the peace that appears

I run from my hiding place, deep in the dying woods
Dive into the warm and clear crystal
The palace of evergreens bursts into an inferno
Tears from my eyes fade to nothing as I rest in a gemstone

I lie in the water as the plain burns
Watch in wonder as my world is destroyed
Then it hits me, has one learned
To extinguish the shadow, find the light?

Sarah Lee (15)
Burnside Community High School, Wallsend

A Potion To Help The Third World

Take some very poor countries
Add clean water, food and shops to buy it from
Pour in a spoonful of medicine
Mix in hospitals, pubs, a swimming pool or two
Then buses and cars, some amusements too
Chop in a market selling clothes and sweets
Toys for the children
And a park to play in
Sprinkle in trees and flowers
With birds above
And don't forget a large measure of love.

Michael Warren (15)
Catcote School, Hartlepool

The Writer Of This Poem

(Based on 'The Writer Of This Poem' by Roger McGough)

The writer of this poem
Is taller than a church
As keen as Linkin Park
As grumpy as can be
As bold as a three ton truck
As sharp as a spike
As strong as a steel pipe
As tricky as a hundred piece puzzle
As smart as a mechanic
As quick as a leopard
As clean as a Dyson.

Ashley Aston (13)
Catcote School, Hartlepool

Recipe For A Millionaire Lifestyle

Take several posh cars
Add one 32 million pund house
Mix in one tennis court
Stir in half a dozen stretch limos
Rub in six elegant bathrooms

Meanwhile, peel 36 bedrooms
Chop one large kitchen
Melt eight reception rooms
Cook one dozen garages
Drain three drawing rooms

Freeze in your extra large garden
Simmer in your silky sleeping bag for one and a half hours
Pour a lovely cup of hot chocolate and
Drink expensive champagne from crystal glasses
While relaxing in your king-size four-poster bed.

Marc Hodge (14)
Catcote School, Hartlepool

A Potion To Annoy The World

First take a bunch of skateboarders
Add strong metal boards
Mix in a drop of evil
Then go into battle
Do stunts, jump and turn
Increase the heat
Terrify people
And terrorise the world.

Alan Juillerat (14)
Catcote School, Hartlepool

The Writer Of This Poem

(Based on 'The Writer Of This Poem' by Roger McGough)

The writer of this poem
Is taller than a tower
As keen as a Man U fan
As handsome as can be
As bold as a bulldog
As sharp as a sword
As strong as a Volvo car
As tricky as a pack of cards
As smart as a pair of brogues
As quick as a flash
As clean as a whistle
As clever as a wizard
The writer of this poem
Never ceases to amaze
He's one in a million
Or so he often says.

Robert Pounder (18)
Catcote School, Hartlepool

One Love Forever

Melt your heart and sweep me off my feet
I will not let you go
Always be faithful and trust me
No need to buy me roses and chocolates
Because I will always love you
Total commitment you to me.

Jane Ducker (14)
Catcote School, Hartlepool

Before The World Began

Cold, still and quiet is the wasteland,
No movement for miles around.
Untouched and peaceful,
Ready and waiting.

A force awakens
Deep in the ground.
Full of energy,
Waiting to shape the Earth.

The ground moans and groans,
Shivers and shakes,
As the force pushes at the Earth's crust.
A small patch of ground moves steadily upwards.

The patch gets taller
The force gets angrier.
It pushes so hard the land begins to shake!
The sun sets on the gradually rising horizon.

Inside the rock begins to bubble and boil,
The patch gets higher until *crack!*
The mountain bursts open and out pours
A golden orange, white-hot liquid.

It spreads over the land,
Reducing everything to cinders.
The new, amazing lava-spitting hill,
Smokes like a dragon.

As the lava turned to rock, new hills were formed,
As fast as a child making sandcastles.
Now the world was ready,
Ready and waiting.

Laura Bland (11)
Central Newcastle High School, Newcastle-Upon-Tyne

The Sands Do Shift

The sands do shift and time flows on
The seasons go by and everything is gone
And all that remains are silent memories
Of whispering winds and raging seas

Tormented souls of forgotten law
Fly on the clouds for evermore
And when our season's over we all fade away
The rain comes down and dawns another day

Until we just exist in a single person's mind
Mourning all the tragic moments we had to leave behind
Then we become nothing more than dust on a rising sun
The stars themselves do tremble and the change has begun

But there will be a time when they remember you and me
This will see the events that were to be
They will see the people form whom they all inherit
Omnia Mutantur Nihil Interit.

Christine Clark (11)
Central Newcastle High School, Newcastle-Upon-Tyne

The Trampolinist

Up, up, up so high,
Almost looks like she can fly.
Twirling, whirling amazing to see,
Moving gracefully like the waves of the sea.
The trampolinist.

Graceful like the birds in the trees,
She moves gently but expertly.
Moving swiftly like the wind in your hair,
Falling gently through the air.
The trampolinist.

Georgina Davison (12)
Central Newcastle High School, Newcastle-Upon-Tyne

Stalker

As the stalker creeps out of its house,
The prey creeps out of its hole,

The stalker creeps round the prey,
The prey cannot see it is too young,

Then the stalker gets ready to attack,
The prey's mum calls out a warning,

The stalker pounces for its food,
The prey runs for its life,

The stalker is angry it's missed its chance,
The prey's mum helps to comfort it,

The cat stalks off inside its house,
The mouse is safe inside its hole.

Emily Cogan (11)
Central Newcastle High School, Newcastle-Upon-Tyne

A Tree In A Storm

Its branches are arms,
Flailing in the wind,
Or is it having a nightmare
And is terrified?
Its leaves are the sound of a badly tuned radio,
Crackling and hissing.
Its trunk is an old man,
Frail and fragile,
The bark is wrinkled skin,
It creeks and grumbles, moans and groans
And complains that its back is sore,

I do not know how long it has stood there,
But I do know,
It does not stand there anymore.

Elspeth Crawford (11)
Central Newcastle High School, Newcastle-Upon-Tyne

Life

Each time a baby is born,
A torch is lit.
As he grows,
So does the torch.
At happy moments,
The torch goes brighter,
When sad,
The torch is dull.
As he becomes older,
The torch's wood becomes gnarled.
When he dies,
The light gets smaller and smaller,
Until only smoke curls up into the sky.
Forgotten,
Gone.

Laura Cuthbertson (12)
Central Newcastle High School, Newcastle-Upon-Tyne

River's Journey

Twisting, twirling,
Whistling, whirling,
Never stopping, always turning,
Comes to the waterfall.
Tension increases,
Water still running,
Never ceases.
Slightly tipping,
Water's dripping,
Plummets over the side,
Lashing, smashing,
Bouncing off the rocks,
Plunges into the tide
And stops.

Holly Elsdon (11)
Central Newcastle High School, Newcastle-Upon-Tyne

Growing Up

I was born on the third of March
And my mum had a big surprise,
Instead of one baby in her tummy,
There were three of us inside!

The toddler stage came next,
What fun that would be,
Instead of one little monster,
My mum and dad had three!

We were never like each other,
But the older we became,
It was obvious to everyone
We weren't at all the same.

Two of us started dancing,
One of us liked sport,
Although we were very different,
We never really fought.

We started school together,
We soon made our own friends,
But the friendship I have with my sisters,
Will never come to an end.

Being born a triplet,
Is very normal to me,
But other people's reactions,
Are as amazing as can be.

The friendship with my sisters,
Is really like no other
And to top off all of this,
I have an older brother!

Megan Shaw (11)
Central Newcastle High School, Newcastle-Upon-Tyne

The Coaster!

Twisting and twirling,
Whirling and whirling,
Up and down we go,
Screaming and shouting,
Louder and louder,
Up and down we go.

People were sicky,
It was quite icky,
Up and down we go,
My tummy was turning
And whirling and whirling,
Up and down we go.

The coaster was slowing
And slowing and slowing,
Down and down we go,
Slower and slower,
Is the ride over?
Down and down we go.

Then we set off again
Twisting and twirling,
Up and down we go,
Twisting and twirling,
Curling and whirling,
On and on we go.

Emma Florek (11)
Central Newcastle High School, Newcastle-Upon-Tyne

A Journey To The Sea

My life began a while ago
When I rose up from the sea,
I felt my body arise up to the sky
Then settle down amongst the clouds.

I stayed still for a week or so
But then I was needed,
It was time to go home again,
Back down to Earth.

Amongst my friends
Down I went,
Everybody hid from me,
They put on special coats, and ran into their homes.

I fell into a stream
And trickled to the sea,
Slowly, I went
As I felt my body sway.

Very soon I was back at home,
Beside the coral and fishes,
This is my home.
To stay for evermore.

I'm a raindrop
And that was my story.

Polly Marlow (11)
Central Newcastle High School, Newcastle-Upon-Tyne

From A Little Acorn . . .

I am a little acorn, a tiny little seed,
Feeling very vulnerable, covered by a weed.
The start of life, my journey's begun,
To grow and grow in the light of the sun.

As the years passed up and up I shoot,
Swaying up above from such a solid root,
Feeling small and tender and trying to grow strong,
I struggle in the changing seasons and some just seem so long.

I sense the same old feeling my bows they stretch right out,
A burst of growth and all around my leaves begin to sprout.
I love this time, how handsome I feel,
My leaves popping, my buds so real.

Shock and horror what's happening to me?
There is someone climbing on this tree,
Swinging and swaying on my branches so weak,
I wonder, I wonder what damage they will wreak,
But wait a minute, they're smiling at me,
It's me they want, I'm their special tree.

I look in despair as my leaves disappear,
They melt into the snow because winter is here.
I am no longer colourful, the children have gone,
As the snow builds on my branches, for spring I deeply long.

As my rings of age get counted, I wonder am I old?
The others think my age they know but to me it remains untold,
I cast a glance below my bow and what do you think I see?
That start of life a tiny acorn staring up at me.

I now look back upon my life and can sum up what I see,
I was a tiny acorn and am now a bold oak tree!

Amy Harrison (12)
Central Newcastle High School, Newcastle-Upon-Tyne

Poetry In Motion

A white dazzling shape, gliding elegantly over the water,
A swan, an English beauty.
Neck long, held up high proudly, tail pointed, perfectly streamlined.
Two webbed feet propel the creature gently across the water.
An animal in motion.

Two hands, moving slowly round a face.
Tick . . . Tock . . .
Big Ben, an English landmark.
Hands pulling towards the numerals.
Tick . . . Tock . . .
Human's getting on with life, unaware that the hands still keep going
round and round.
Tick . . . Tock . . .
A machine in motion.

Floating gently, a passenger on the breeze,
Sun streaming through the material.
The British flag.
Red, white and blue can be seen rippling proudly across the sky,
A flag to be waved joyfully, born to billow in the wind.
An object in motion.

An English daisy,
Always turning towards the sun,
Roots always searching, spreading, trying to find water.
Petals opening out to welcome the sun,
Closing back up at night, keeping out the dark.
Nature in motion.

Rebecca Jameson (11)
Central Newcastle High School, Newcastle-Upon-Tyne

Sunflower

Plant a seed in spring
Patience and hope
Eagerly waiting
Will my flower grow?

Spy a shoot
Green tip emerges
From beneath the soil
Watch it grow.

Summer now, radiant sun
Basking in the heat
Day by day, inch by inch
My sunflower grows taller and taller.

A yellow face
Opens out
Tilts towards the sun
Smiling, enjoying the summer days.

Too soon autumn arrives
The happy face now old and sad
It droops and withers
Nothing last forever.

Rose Hodgson (11)
Central Newcastle High School, Newcastle-Upon-Tyne

Mother Nature

Trees, swaying in the cool, calm breeze
The leaves, stirring in the wind.
Flowers, slowly springing out from their buds
Their vibrant colours making an illusion on the pale background.
The rivers, rippling away to the beat of the air
The fishes gliding away in unison.
The grass a perfect shade of green, coated with drops of dew.
The sun shines high above this unspoiled beauty
Whilst Mother Nature casts her spell.

Anupriya Singh (12)
Central Newcastle High School, Newcastle-Upon-Tyne

All In A Year

High on the hillside, alone I stand
My branches are bare and my trunk is numb.
The frost has frozen everything in sight,
But there is hope yet for spring is to come.

My leaves delicately unfold,
As I watch the daffodils dancing around my feet.
The beautiful sound of the song thrush breaks the silence.
All the animals frolic in pairs.
Life itself has returned.

The heat of the summer builds like a fever
Dazzling, rich colours of the beautiful roses are at their best.
The children's joy is clear as they climb my branches.
These endless days are indeed happy days.

My leaves have begun to yellow, and soon they will fall,
The sound of the songbird is fading,
The animals are entering a long sleep.

I must prepare, the long, cold winter is nearly here.

Amaani Hussain (11)
Central Newcastle High School, Newcastle-Upon-Tyne

The Blinking Eye

The eye is always watching,
Waiting for a tear to come,
Then it will blink,
Slowly letting the tear pass,
Returns to its original place,
With a flutter of its lashes.

A cease in the flow of cyclists and pedestrians,
A momentary pause,
The boats wait for it to swing,
The hydraulic pumps come to life,
The bridge sways, the eye opens,
The ships sail beneath.

Sophie R Robertson (11)
Central Newcastle High School, Newcastle-Upon-Tyne

The Bird's Journey

Swooping, gliding, diving, singing,
The bird flies through the air,
Flitting, fluttering, soaring, smiling,
Harmony is everywhere.

All around is paradise; nothing is out of place,
Luscious, green pastures and wonderful pure streams.
Flowers and fruits of all colours and shapes,
Are enjoyed in the summer sun.
Everything is peaceful and perfect, yet still full of life.

The bird flies on . . .

Swooping, gliding, diving, coughing,
The bird flies through the air.
Flitting, fluttering, soaring, frowning,
Harmony is nowhere.

All around is the sickly smell of fumes
And the sound of poor trees falling.
Clouds of smoke are polluting the air,
Clunking machines are scaring the animals.
Everything is sickening and smelly, nothing is welcomed at all.

The poor bird asks herself, what have humans done?

Jane Stockdale (11)
Central Newcastle High School, Newcastle-Upon-Tyne

Poetry In Motion

The soldiers are marching proudly for their country.
The gymnasts are training practising their flips, splits and more.

The Union Jack is flapping in the cold London breeze.
The Queen is waving from the balcony of Buckingham Palace.

The drop of the oblivion, at the theme park Alton Towers.
The excitement of shopping as you run about Harvey Nichols.

This is how I think of poetry in motion.

Sophie Winter (11)
Central Newcastle High School, Newcastle-Upon-Tyne

Rivers Flowing

R ivers are wet, rivers are flowing.
I n the night, rivers are glowing.
V alleys steep, valleys short,
E verywhere, they can't get caught.
R ivers are wet, rivers are flowing
S omewhere even the rocks are showing.

F loods are deep, floods are strong,
L apping over the windows and doors.
O ver the tables, over the chairs,
W ater takes over, the floors are all bare.
I n the night, the catastrophe starts,
N obody aware of the trouble ahead.
G oing quickly towards them, they can't escape.
　　Because it's too late.

Chantal Yeung (12)
Central Newcastle High School, Newcastle-Upon-Tyne

Growing Up

Growing up is such a pain,
Sometimes it drives you insane.
Friends became enemies so fast,
Every day you have a good blast.
You spend all your money and need more pay
And you can never get your own way.

Parents always nagging at you
And always wanting to know what's new.
Girls and boys start noticing each other,
Seeing them without telling their mother.

And homework and school is the worst of all,
Teachers giving you homework until you fall.
I'm sure everyone will get fed up,
Especially with growing up!

Laura Calvert (13)
Dyke House School, Hartlepool

Life . . .

Life is short
Don't waste it
You have enemies
You have friends

Life is weird
With its ups
And its downs
Don't let anyone get in your way
Nor get you down

Respect your friends
Your family
Your world
Don't waste the time you have
Don't waste your life.

Adam Hinks (13)
Dyke House School, Hartlepool

Death

I can remember that fatal day
Waking up to a bright sunny morning,
Looking forward to the day ahead,
Until I found my brother's goldfish dead.

I remember him getting out of bed
Bouncing down the stairs,
To walk into the front room,
To find his goldfish dead.

He cried and cried all day and night,
Wishing it as there in its bowl, swimming
On that fatal day,
The goldfish died.

Anthony Heron (13)
Dyke House School, Hartlepool

Life

Life to me is fifty-fifty,
One minute you're drowning in sorrow and pain,
It may have been the loss of a friend,
Or a death of a relative.

Next your happiness machine is on overload,
A new member has just joined your family,
You are now officially a grandparent.

You are growing very old now,
The new member of the family is going through childhood,
Then through boyhood,
He goes to high school as a teenager.

You're *dead!*
Everyone is drowning in sorrow and pain,
A relative of theirs has died,
Then comes a new member of the family.

Matthew Price (13)
Dyke House School, Hartlepool

Special Things In Life

The best things in life,
Are your friends,
They're there through trouble and strife,
They'll be there day and night,
They'll never ever leave your side until the day your friendship's died.

Another special thing in life, are your best friends your family,
They comfort you, they worship you, they care about you most,
They're there for you no matter what
And will always hold you close.

Emma Calvert (13)
Dyke House School, Hartlepool

Life

Life
People born
People live
People die
Life goes on

People cause
Suffering and pain
Even though
There isn't much to gain

It doesn't stop
It doesn't alter
People dying
But the armies never falter

Life is special
Life is good
People behaving
Like they should

Life is love
Life is great
But people are filled
With so much hate.

Kimberley White (13)
Dyke House School, Hartlepool

Hartlepool

Hartlepool is a really nice town
Our football team is up and down.
Historic quay and marina too
There's lots of things for us to do
We play and fish to pass the day
And watch the boats as they sail away
So if you come to see the quay
Please make sure you're not a monkey.

Chris Charlton (13)
Dyke House School, Hartlepool

Divine Sorrow

By the age of four
They put me into care
Ripped my heart out
Laughed at me while down

Through and through
Till I was eight
Lived with nice
Foster family

Then they said goodbye
On my eighth birthday party
Left my brothers behind
Never to see again

Moved to Hartlepool
Went to public school
Realised the coldness
Of the world

Now my mother
Wants to reunite
The one who gave
Me up to misery

My father wants
To see me the same
Man who beat me
And almost killed me

They put me through
Misery
So now it goes back to them

What should
I say
Am I to
Run away?

Gemma Sharpe (13)
Dyke House School, Hartlepool

Life

Life - so what?

You're born,
You live a little,
You die.

It's as simple as that.

You suck a bottle,
Cry a bit,
Sleep.

It's as simple as that.

You make friends,
Make enemies,
Grow up.

It's as simple as that.

You get married,
Argue,
Get divorced.

It's as simple as that.

You get old,
Get wrinkly,
Get ill.
It's as simple as that.

Jade Ainsley (13)
Dyke House School, Hartlepool

Hartlepool

Sunshine and beaches give me a smile
Big shopping centre worth the while
Sea is cloudy, full of life
Toxic waste under the knife
Great nightlife to die for
Bad people breaking the law
This is Hartlepool, better beware.

Craig Lythe (14)
Dyke House School, Hartlepool

Black And White

He walks in the night,
He hides in the day,
He is the secret force that no one sees
But everyone suffers from.
He has no physical form
That he can turn the arrow
Of integrity, as he tries to save a soul.
He inhabits the deepest recesses of the weak minded,
The insignificant, the disliked,
Offers other human beings
For one small price
Their unity and peace with all men.
He uses them to sweep down
On a shadow in the light.
Biting, kicking, stabbing.
Mercilessly, he feeds on every scream,
Every plea.
The shadow turns to red.
He swallows every drop of blood.
His minions of the white side shed.
Then the vessel for his hatred is left for dead.
He is the division between
Light and dark.
One more for the light side.

Emma Swainson (13)
Dyke House School, Hartlepool

Pain

Eating me from the inside,
Pills are just a selling point,
They don't relieve me,
Make me whole again,
This feeling is torture,
Killing
And I can't do anything about it.

Steven Smurthwaite (13)
Dyke House School, Hartlepool

Depression

Depression,
It eats away at you from the inside,
Like a horrifying disease,
Just keeps eating and eating away
Until
There's nothing left, until you're
Empty,
No feelings, no heart,
Nothing. . .
Makes you want to cut yourself,
There's a little voice inside your head,
Saying, 'Go on, go on, it will only
hurt for a
Little bit!'

Shaun Foxon (13)
Dyke House School, Hartlepool

Soldier

Should I go or should I stay?
Who knows? I don't.
Thoughts and ideas go through my head.
What is war? Why does war happen?
That's a question nobody can really answer.
But at the end of the day war has to happen.
I have to go, I have to.
I'm 17, enthusiastic and raring to go.
I've got nobody to worry about,
Nobody to worry about me.
I'm a lean mean SAS soldier with nothing to lose.

Matthew Forcer (13)
Dyke House School, Hartlepool

Hartlepool Poem

Hartlepool is a town in the North East,
People in it are real beasts.

It has a really nice marina,
Shopping centre and football arena.

I've lived here all my life,
I've lived through so much trouble and strife.

In Hartlepool, one half is sea and tide,
The other side we have some countryside.

So you see, Hartlepool is really nice,
If you come here once you'll come here twice.

Daniel Begley (14)
Dyke House School, Hartlepool

Hartlepool Is . . .

Hartlepool is the world of history
From museums to ships to art

Hartlepool is the place for scenic views
From high up to see all around

Hartlepool is the place where shopping counts
In every shop is a bargain

Hartlepool is where the arcades are best
From Seaside Sammy's to Las Vegas

Hartlepool owns Seaton beach
Which won best beach in the 1960s.

Nicola Robinson (13)
Dyke House School, Hartlepool

Hartlepool

As I strolled down Seaton front licking my ice cream
I was astonished by the weather, it was sweltering
My back was burning with the heat
As I slowly kicked the calm, cool sand with my feet.
I then decided to go to the marina
As I saw the fantastic views
My eyes were then glued to this big, bold bay
In the middle of a roundabout.

Shannon Davis (13)
Dyke House School, Hartlepool

Hartlepool

The sun glistening on the sea
People playing on the sandy beaches
The yachts swaying in the wind

Children playing in the sea
The marina shining in the sun
The sea calmly settling down

The waves smoothly turning over
A wonderful day at Hartlepool.

Jonathan Hill (14)
Dyke House School, Hartlepool

Hartlepool

Sitting on the coastline
Sea lapping on the shore
Hartlepool, a lively place
History galore!
Views that go out to sea
Ships that sail one by one
Come and visit the Trincomalee
Hartlepool, Hartlepool, the place to be.

Kathryn Hall (13)
Dyke House School, Hartlepool

The Young And The Hopeless

'You're hopeless,'
That's what everyone says,
I'm only a teenager
Only young.

I sometimes wonder,
Why do people call me
Hopeless,
Young and hopeless?

How am I hopeless?
I can do things,
Help out,
I'm not that young either.

Do this, do that,
I get told every day,
If I refuse,
The answer I get is
'You're hopeless.'

You see teenagers,
Who don't do anything,
Who sit around
All day.
When I see people like that,
I say,
'Now that's what I call
The young and the hopeless.'

Leanne Whitelock (13)
Dyke House School, Hartlepool

John Andy

In 1855 there was a thief
He stole some cotton wool
He was kicked out of town
Because he thought he was cool

The law knew him well
He was called John Andy
After a big robbery
The town was very angry

He was very clever
He stole lots of gold
He was the cleverest
He wore a hat because he was bald

He went to live in the woods
Andy stole and gave it to the poor
They loved him very much
But the rich thought he was cruel

He lived with the poor
A year later he fell in love
He lived happily ever after
All the rich thought he was gone.

Xhul Islami (12)
Eston Park School, Middlesbrough

Winter Poem

The snow falls all around,
The robin outside whistling a sound.

Writing out my Christmas list,
The sun is out there in the mist.

Waking up on Christmas morning,
Christmas Day is never boring.

When winter's over, all is done,
I cannot wait for spring to come.

Rachel Gregory (12)
Eston Park School, Middlesbrough

The Awoken Kraken

We rose above the world
Wind blowing in our faces
People down below like sticks
My feet hanging from the midday sky

We reached the top
I couldn't turn back
We started to go
The kraken took over

The kraken roared
Like a fierce lion
The muscular creature
Had awoken

Sharp turns here and there
I had no control
Us people had no effect
Over the incredible sea creature.

John Thrower (12)
Eston Park School, Middlesbrough

Careless Carl

Careless Carl from Teesville, in 1864
Was thrown out in the rain,
Told not to come back anymore

In the fight that followed
He laid the governor down
Before getting on his horse
And riding out of town

Knocks on any farmer's door
He tells his life story
But no one finds him a bore.

Carl Wilson (12)
Eston Park School, Middlesbrough

Jackass Jay

This is an unhappy story about
Jackass Jay on the run
This all happened years ago
In the town of Nottingham.

When he robbed a bank
In the year 1804,
When he was shutting the vault door,
He lost his toe.

When escaping he hit the chief
And killed a little pain
He escaped on a horse
And the chase was in vain.

Some people cried and some people denied
But in the court he was hung
He lived his life as he wanted to
Always carrying his gun.

James Eades (12)
Eston Park School, Middlesbrough

Seasonal Haikus

Springtime is now here
Green buds start to appear now
Flowers start to grow

Summertime is great
The sun shining way up high
Blue sky all around.

It's autumn again
Leaves get sprinkled on the ground
Strong winds blow around.

Winter is coming
Prepare for the cold weather
Snow could be falling.

Abi Winton-Wright (12)
Eston Park School, Middlesbrough

Silly Kelly

Silly Kelly got shot out of town,
In the year of 1509,
She fell out with the mean sheriff
And was blamed for every crime.

She had ginger hair,
She looked like a beast,
She was quite nasty
And her boyfriend was a priest.

I know she was silly,
I know she was cruel,
I know she was a bully,
But her mam thought she was cool.

Silly Kelly saved her sister,
From drowning in the pool,
Everyone saw her unselfish act,
To prove that she wasn't cruel.

Silly Kelly loved her sister,
She told her every day,
They decided together,
That the sheriff was going to pay.

Kelly Stephenson (12)
Eston Park School, Middlesbrough

Milo

My dog was black
And he was called Milo.
He was only three, but nearly four
And his birthday was in November.
He had a heater for winter
To keep him nice and warm
And a beanbag to snuggle up in
When he was frightened of the storms!

Ashleigh Hannah (12)
Eston Park School, Middlesbrough

Sammo Samantha

Sammo Samantha got shot out of the street,
For staying out all night
And for always getting into arguments,
She was always in a fight.

She had long, blonde hair
And sparkling blue eyes,
She looked like a ghost
And she always spied.

She was dangerous,
She was very mad,
She was so crazy,
But she was never sad.

She stole from a bank,
She stole lots of money,
She was very poor,
Now isn't that funny?

She didn't have any money,
Because she gave it all away,
No one she knew went hungry,
Everyone had a place to stay.

Samantha Stephenson (12)
Eston Park School, Middlesbrough

Red Eye Rawles The Outlaw

Red Eye Rawles the outlaw,
Bottle of whiskey in his hand,
Got thrown out of Eston,
So he went a-roaming across the land.

It's up to you if you believe me,
This story is very old,
The sheriff caught Red Eye Rawles,
With a thousand pounds in gold.

Red Eye Rawles the outlaw,
He said the sheriff was lying,
The sheriff didn't know what to do,
So he got chucked out of town for crying.

Red Eye Rawles the outlaw,
No one saw him with the swag,
But he always had a funny frown,
So they said that he was bad.

Red Eye Rawles the outlaw,
Was allowed back in town,
One day the sheriff called him a thief,
So he laid that sheriff down.

Lewis Rawles (12)
Eston Park School, Middlesbrough

The Beast From The East

The sun was shining in the sky,
She looked down on the world from high
And what she saw moved through the land,
Destroying trees, throwing sand.

When the mountains were informed,
They saw the creature, 'twas deformed,
A shadow moving from the east,
A monster not of man, but beast.

The armies of men, then were told,
The greatest force of history old,
They fought a battle, long and hard,
Now comes the truly heroic part,
A man called Martin, fearless soldier,
More than any other, bolder,
Drove his sword into its shoulder.

No more of beast or man is known,
Both fighters sit not on the throne,
Of ancient Europe none do own,
But from that battle evil seeds were sown.

Sam Sanderson (13)
Eston Park School, Middlesbrough

There Was A Young Man From Dorset

There was a young man from Dorset,
Who always wore a pink corset,
He decided to wear a red frock
And thought it would look nice with a black sock,
Then he wore it one night for a bet.

He was always so drunk,
He smelt like a skunk,
He was sick on the floor
And all up the door,
Then was no longer a gorgeous hunk!

Emily McPartland (12)
Eston Park School, Middlesbrough

Winter

The crisp, clean freshness on my face,
lets me know that I'm free.
As I'm walking through the snow,
I see a robin in a tree.
As I look up at him,
he smiles back at me.

I make footprints in the snow,
to hear the crunch beneath my feet.
Where it takes me I don't know,
it's so cold but I feel heat.

A snow storm is coming,
as the wind starts to blow
and on my face it does show.
With flakes on my tongue and chattering teeth,
so red are my cheeks and blue is my nose,
this is home for me I suppose.

Gemma Havelock (13)
Eston Park School, Middlesbrough

I Am . . .

I am bad, vile, unpleasant,
I am a rogue, a tramp, a brute,
I am darkness, destruction and death,
I am king of the damned and undead,
I am evil, infection and sorrow.

I lurk in the shadows,
No light for me,
The shadows give my strength
And the brightness draws it.

I shall bring upon a plague of death,
All good shall disappear,
I shall bring upon Ragnarok,
Or as you call it,
Armageddon.

Lee Keenan (12)
Eston Park School, Middlesbrough

The Storm

The storm was raging,
The trees were ageing.
The rain was torrential,
Fulfilling its potential.

The lightning was bright,
It lit up the night.
The thunder rumbled,
As the bees had once bumbled.

Suddenly silence,
There was no more violence.
Out came the sun,
It was time for fun.

The kids came running,
The birds started humming.
Outside to play,
It was a lovely day.

The storm was over,
Yes the storm was over
It had its attack
And it won't be back.

Liane McGovern (13)
Eston Park School, Middlesbrough

Limericks Of The UK

There was a young man from Wales,
Who thought that he would sail.
He slipped on the deck
And broke his neck,
Then got his head stuck in a pail.

There was an old woman from Aberdeen,
Who turned totally green.
She hid in a shed,
With a bag on her head,
As she didn't want to be seen.

There was a young woman from Leeds,
Who swallowed a packet of seeds.
She thought she'd have power,
As a giant sunflower,
Then realised she'd swallowed some weeds.

There was an old man from Dublin,
Who tripped and got stuck in a bin.
He started to shout
And finally got out,
Then tripped and fell back in.

Tanya Davison (12)
Eston Park School, Middlesbrough

Limericks

There was a young man from Leeds
Who ate some garden seeds
He drank some water
And told his daughter
That from his mouth grew weeds.

There was a young man called Fred
Who was too fat to get out of bed
He lay watching the telly
But he couldn't see for his belly
'Exercise I need,' Fred said.

There was once a woman called Kelly
Who lived in an extremely large welly
Most things were large too
Including her dog, Sue
So there was no room for a telly.

Rosie Stockil (12)
Eston Park School, Middlesbrough

Mildred's Mad Mum!

There once was a lass called Mildrid,
Who dated a guy named Sid,
Her mother hated that scrawny boy, so this is what she did:
One day in the middle of June,
Her mother invited him round and the couple sat under the moon.
Mildred's mother came out and picked up Sid,
Whoosh, she threw him up to space, she did.
So think before you invite round your boyfriend and show him
                                          to your mum,
You might well say she's the maddest mum under the sun!
It's better than your boyfriend being hauled into space,
If you have a mother like Mildred's - a total *nutcase!*

Emma Todd (12)
Eston Park School, Middlesbrough

Seasons

Winter is a cold time
When snowflakes hit the ground
Sharp and pointy icicles
Come all season round.

Autumn is a crispy time
When leaves start to die
Children come out of their houses
And into the leaves they dive.

Summer is a warm time
When children break from school
They take out their paddling pools
Just to keep cool.

My favourite season of them all
Has to be spring
Because out come the flowers
And animal lives begin.

Nicola Jones (12)
Eston Park School, Middlesbrough

Creature

I sit on my rock
I change colour to match it
The chameleon

I am so angry
Like an enormous man-beast
I am the tiger

I slither around
On my very sleek stomach
The slippery snake

I hope in the wild
I love to eat some carrots
I am the rabbit.

Michael Cockerill (12)
Eston Park School, Middlesbrough

The Gangly Man

Think of a place
As dark as you can
As dark as the hut
Of the gangly man!
Who lives off fried peanuts
And seaweed on toast
To see him
Would surely frighten a ghost
His fingers are thin
And yet so strong
That he can pick winkles
The whole year long
A long twig-like nose
And large yellow eyes
And when someone comes near
They double in size
In the seaside resort
Where the gangly man lives
He gets his reward
For the fun that he gives
Tickets appear
From the shadows inside
Of the gangly man's hut
On the ghost train ride.

Fenella Charles (12)
Eston Park School, Middlesbrough

A Trip To The Beauticians

When I go to the beauty salon,
My auntie paints my nails,
A file and polish does the trick,
But quitting biting fails.

She always puts on my make-up,
In fifty different ways,
And when she finally finishes,
I stand there unamazed.

Next up it is the facial,
To wake up all those heads,
She's going to need to work and work,
To get them out of bed.

Oh dear here's the waxing,
I'm going to scream in vain,
Pretty please do stop hurting me,
I cannot stand the pain.

I look forward to the best bit,
It is not harsh or mean,
The body relaxing massage,
I'm now a beauty queen.

Jessica Harrison (12)
Eston Park School, Middlesbrough

The Snow Princess

She sleeps in the snow,
Her wings made from ice and crystal,
Her crown made from jewels,
Wrapped up in a cocoon,
Waiting for him to come,
Her only chance to wake.

She's seen him in her dreams,
But not in reality,
Her lips are frosted together,
Only he can break the spell,
She's still waiting for him to come,
Her only chance to wake.

She's all alone,
Embedded in the soft white sheets,
A red rose lays in her fingers,
He had put it there before,
Promised he'd see her soon,
But she's still waiting for him to come,
He's her only chance to wake.

A hundred years had passed,
A prince approached the show,
Where his true love he had left
And now he was here, now she wasn't waiting,
Now she could wake.

He had stumbled over rocks,
Climbed the highest mountains,
To awake his snow princess,
But when he touched her soft, snowy lips,
She was still sleeping, always sleeping,
    Dead!

Lucy Yeomans (12)
Eston Park School, Middlesbrough

A Winter's Day

This winter's day was a cheerful day,
As me and my steed carried on our way.
The snow glistening in the last light,
Taking in the rays of the new night,
I went for a walk in the woods today.

This cold winter's night,
With a glimpse of moonlight,
Will guide me on my way
To a cup of hot chocolate
And somewhere to stay.
Guess who was walking through the woods today?

A tired winter's day it has been,
The woods, a perfect painter's scene.
Snow crunching below my steed,
Perfect harmony, a flower, not a weed.
I was walking in the woods that day.

A beautiful winter's day today.
Myself, I have travelled quite a way.
I am tired, so is my horse,
From travelling this way, day after day.
I was walking through the woods today.

A long winter's day today.
The snow untouched on the ground it lay.
Watching a squirrel,
My horse pawed the ground.

A long winter's day it has been,
A wood, distant, but seen.
My horse drowsy,
But I am happy,
Walking through the woods that day.

Helen Gavillet (12)
Eston Park School, Middlesbrough

All Four Seasons

The flowers appear,
spring is here,
the lambs are young,
spring has sprung,
everyone is full of good cheer.

Summer is nigh,
hooray we cry,
sea and sand,
go hand in hand,
the sun high up in the sky.

Leaves are falling off the trees,
in the strong but cold breeze,
on the trees there is not a lot
and it's not very hot,
soon lakes will freeze.

Wintertime is here,
time to get out the beer,
Christmas trees are put up,
so grab your cup
and fill up with Christmas cheer!

Lauren Doddy (12)
Eston Park School, Middlesbrough

People In The Clouds

Clouds are like animals and plants,
designed in every shape.
Sometimes you see different people,
that all live together.

They follow the world round and round,
and sometimes they go on holiday,
every day there are different people,
and every day I look into the sky
just to see what people and animals are there,
but I never see the same people.

Joanne Taylor (12)
Eston Park School, Middlesbrough

Johnny Brown

This is a story of Johnny Brown,
The meanest outlaw in the land,
He stole from babies, children and grannies,
So that his bank balance would expand.

He stole the mayor's daughter,
Just so he could have her pounds,
Then he went to the bank,
And got caught out of bounds.

Then he was in court,
He got put in jail,
Then he denied it,
And got let out on bail.

When he was let out,
The mayor's daughter he did wed,
When the mayor heard of this,
He shot poor Johnny dead.

Josh Groves (12)
Eston Park School, Middlesbrough

Season Haikus

Spring is here at last,
Baby lambs are being born,
New flowers blossom.

Summer has begun,
The sun is shining brightly,
Everyone's happy.

Autumn has arrived,
Crisp red leaves are all around,
Blowing with the wind.

Winter has begun,
It is very cold outside,
Nights are closing in.

Rachel Rowland (12)
Eston Park School, Middlesbrough

Dean, Dean, The Killing Machine

Dean, Dean, the killing machine
The outlaw of the west
Everyone knew him very well
So he shot the sheriff in the chest

When Dean got angry
His face went beetroot-red
He lay in a worn out shack
And slept on a rickety bed

He had a pet mouse called Fred
Who he blamed for all of his crimes
Especially the great cheese robbery
Of 1899

Despite Dean's trap
The mouse ran away
Dean had used the wrong cheese
The mouse is still running free today.

Dean Evans (12)
Eston Park School, Middlesbrough

Music Haiku

Jamming to the beat
Playing on the stereo
Liking it a lot

Turn the music up
To the max so we can hear
Dancing all night long

The dancing goes on
Swing those hips like you don't care
The night is still young.

Hayley Byrne (13)
Eston Park School, Middlesbrough

My Call

Wherever, however, whoever you are
Children and adults, near and far
Just spare a minute to hear my call
If I don't speak out our world will fall

When you next sit down to eat
Or take advantage of a rarer treat
Just remember what I'm telling you
You and I both know it's true

When you next see on TV
The poorer lands and poverty
Just think back to what you've got
Compared to others you've got a lot

And when your family come to call
Don't take advantage of them at all
Some people don't even have one relation
But you can help call out to the nation

The only thing you would have to do
Is spare even only a pound or two
Or help a charity raise money
It's really as easy as one, two, three

Or if that you're not inclined to do
Just write an appeal to see me through
Don't forget what I've just told you
You and I both know it's true.

Beth Cochran (12)
Eston Park School, Middlesbrough

Monkey Madness Michael

Monkey Madness Michael
Lived in a scruffy old house
People blamed him for everything
But he was as quiet as a mouse

It was eighteen fifty-four
When he was accused
His dad was very angry
His mam was not amused

He was in the wrong place at the wrong time
People said he fired the gun
He was two hundred miles away
When the fight begun

He was walking down the street
He saw a very rich lady
All the money she had
Make Monkey Michael crazy

When he saw the money
He just fell in love
He just couldn't believe it
He knew he'd got a bud.

Michael Kirkham (12)
Eston Park School, Middlesbrough

Sewerside Stacey

Sewerside Stacey
Was born in 1945,
For she was an outlaw,
'Surprisingly she's still alive.'

She murdered a man,
Whose name was Larry,
Because she proposed,
He wouldn't marry.

She stole from a bank,
Then got put in jail,
Then she denied it,
She got let out on bail.

Sewerside Stacey saved her sister,
From drowning in a pool,
She went round town,
Everyone thought she was cool.

She robbed a bank,
She murdered a man,
Was thrown out of town,
And roamed the land.

Stacey Wright (12)
Eston Park School, Middlesbrough

Wishes Don't Come True

When the stars came out at night,
He always thought of you,
He thought it through and realised,
That wishes don't come true.

The first star that came into sight,
He made a wish for you,
That someday, somehow, in some way,
He'd always be with you.

But days went by and nights went by,
He kept his wish for you,
And he kept his eyes wide open,
But there was no sign of you.

Sometimes he thought he heard you laugh,
Or say a thing or two,
Sometimes he thought he caught your scent,
In a breeze that was flowing through.

He wished for you a thousand times,
Cried a million tears too,
And then he finally knew inside,
That wishes don't come true.

Nicola Jones (12)
Eston Park School, Middlesbrough

Crazy Killing Kate

The year was 1855,
It was an awful date,
People cried and cried
Because of the anger and hate.

She looked like a witch,
With her long black hair,
If you ever go near her,
You'd better beware.

Kate was very fierce,
With her scary red eyes,
She always killed people,
And nobody was surprised.

People say she's mad,
People say she's crazy,
She killed ten men,
But she saved a baby.

But because she killed ten men,
And she looked like a witch,
She got burned at the stake,
And was buried in a ditch.

Rebecca McAllister (12)
Eston Park School, Middlesbrough

Keenan The Killer!

His name was Keenan the Killer
In 1978 he was around
He made one little mistake
And was thrown out of town.

He tried to save the sheriff
When a crocodile threatened his life
But the bullet ricocheted
And hit the sheriff's wife.

He tried to help an old lady
In her struggle to cross the street
He did not see a truck coming
And now she is dead meat.

So they called him Killer
And he had to run away
He got the blame for every crime
When he was two hundred miles away.

He only wanted to do good deeds
But everything went wrong
If you're out late one night
You might hear him sing his song.

Paul Keenan (12)
Eston Park School, Middlesbrough

A Special Child

This child was brought from the Lord above,
She will need a lot of love.
She may not walk or come to play,
Her thoughts may seem very far away.
In many ways she won't adapt,
She'll be known as handicapped.

Trisha Purvis (15)
George Stephenson High School, Tyne & Wear

Is Life Worth Living I Wonder?

Is life worth living I wonder?
I sat under the ageing sycamore tree, thinking back on my life,
The warm golden sun was slowly fading as it set behind the hills,
I wish I were the sun, just shining above the rest.

I wonder how my life will change in years to come,
Will it be a never-ending tunnel where I'm falling?
Is life worth living I wonder?
A few leaves fell from the tree and I thought that was me.

I got up slowly, the night air had turned cold and I started to shiver,
I looked down at my feet and saw a colony of ants working as a family,
I asked myself, would I have a family like that? Then a horrible
                                              thought hit me,

Will I just fade away when I'm old?
Will I not be noticed?
Is life worth living I wonder?

Is life a word people exaggerate to make it sound perfect?
Life sounds dull, will someone make it worthwhile?

I set off to my home, I could see smoke from my village,
Through the windows I could see families,
They were happy,
Everyone looked warm and cosy,
Why can't my life be like that?
I could see my house now.

As I strolled up to the door, I decided that I was going to make
                                              something of myself,
Life should be exciting; the people who exaggerated it knew what
                                              life could be like,

Is life worth living I wonder?
Yes.

Claire Scott (12)
George Stephenson High School, Tyne & Wear

The Snowy Owls In Flight

Feathers fluttering;
A small white star in the black sky.
An animal of power,
A danger and threat
To all shrews, mice and insects alike.

The silence of its wings,
The lower it goes the more deadly it becomes;
Wings stretched back,
Claws ready to grab,
The eyes locked on the unsuspecting target.

Suddenly it strikes,
The prey never knew what was watching it.
A deadly predator.
It flies back to its tree
Where its youngster is lying,
Waiting to have its dinner.
A caring mother, yet a deadly killer.

Jasmin McKenzie (11)
George Stephenson High School, Tyne & Wear

Life

Life
Life as we know
Goes from stop to go
We all share our life with the bestest of friends
And boys drive girls round the bend
Girls think boys are annoying
Boys think girls are there for annoying
But we all enjoy each other in some way.

Life
Life as we know goes from stop to go
To stop to go, to stop to go, to stop
So if you don't stop annoying each other
You might just stop.

Charlotte Harrison (12)
George Stephenson High School, Tyne & Wear

Stars Sparkle For Me

Can you see the stars at night?
Each little star reminds me of one,
One that has gone before the daylight.
Stars are like sapphires,
Beaming so bright.

Stars can show you the way in the cold, shivering night.
Stars are like an army of bright shining knights
Coming to rescue you
From the dark, gloomy sights.

Stars remind me of people dancing in a big blue ballroom
That twinkles with all its might
To one's eye for the glowing light.

The stars are having a race,
A race around the moon.
Who can shine the brightest of the pack?
Watch the nights
As the stars sparkle with all their might,
With all their light
As they go down.

Stars hovering from far beyond sight,
For one more time
They say goodnight.

Chelsea Kingston (12)
George Stephenson High School, Tyne & Wear

The Sun And Moon

As the day draws in to an end
We watch the bright golden sun
Go down like a balloon.
The glittering moon slowly rises up
And we have fun like we have never had before.
We think of the shimmering sun as it sets in the sky
And dream of the times to come.
We paint the beautiful moon and glittering sun
As we climb to the top of the hill we think of
Our day and wish we could start it again.
Sadly our day is done and all we can do is
Dream of tomorrow.

Ashleigh Lyon (12)
George Stephenson High School, Tyne & Wear

For The One I Love

The silvery light of the moon shines down,
You hold me close and you hold me long,
When I am with you I never wear a frown,
I truly believe our love is not wrong.

Your kisses are sweet and your hugs are warm,
You make me feel funny when you hold me tight,
If you ever leave me my heart will be torn,
I cannot believe how you are so right.

You know that I love you, you know that I do,
You know I need you or forever I'll be blue,
I know for a fact that you love me too,
I'll love you forever, I promise it's true.

I love you so much; I love you my dear,
For when I am with you I see no fear.

Kylie Wood (15)
King Edward VI High School, Morpeth

Tears Of Pearl

As her life flickered
Like a snuffed-out candle,
As the shadows won,
And sun set on the morn,
Angels threw down their haloes
And wept tears of pearl.

Birds fled to shelter,
And foxes went to ground.
As peals of thunder
And lightning did scare,
Angels threw down their haloes
And wept tears of pearl.

Upon the high hill
Where a spirit stood tall,
Dusk fought for freedom,
And her last breath was caught, as
Angels threw down their haloes
And wept tears of pearl.

Emma Hodgkinson (15)
King Edward VI High School, Morpeth

Flowery Power

Why does a single flower,
Lie in front of my face?
Am I really sour,
Or am I full of grace?

Do I make you cower,
Start running for a race,
Running for an hour,
Without a single trace?

Why does a single flower,
Lie in front of my face?
Am I really sour,
Or am I full of grace?

Or do I give you power,
In every single place?
Does love over tower?
Is love what you embrace?

So why is a single flower,
Standing there in front of my face?
Does it say I'm sour,
Or say I'm filled with grace?

Katie Thomas (14)
Macmillan College, Middlesbrough

Infinity Trap

When a door is not a door
A wall turned into space,
The passage (where the passage was)
Has vanished without trace,
When time is made to travel,
Travel time and through the earth,
Thoughts and memories brought to life and made to work.

When you pass into a world
Where somehow all your dreams come true,
All around you seems so distant,
The only real thing is you,
But it is all too real,
Another thing that's real is pain,
And people fight and argue just the same.

You know that you are dreaming,
But you're not in control,
Someone else has taken over,
You hear your own death knell toll
You have to leave, you must get out,
Before your time is up,
And everything around you starts to *stop*.

Bethany Longstaff (14)
Macmillan College, Middlesbrough

Why I Hide My Face

'Why do you hide your face?' they say.
'I hurt,' I say inside.
'I've hurt for so long, I don't remember
When exactly, or how it began.
But I know it was people like you.
Like you, that pulled the trigger.
That struck me a blow to my heart.
That scarred me.

And though the wound may heal,
The flesh renew,
That bullet is buried within,
Too deep in my heart to cast away,
But sometimes, sometimes I try.'

So when they ask, 'Why won't you smile?'
I tell them:
'I am the girl with a heart that cries,
Each time you call my name.
For that is the girl with a broken mind,
And a heart that's nought but sorrow.
I am the girl whose eyes can't smile,
And whose laugh plays automatic.

I am the girl with a heart that cries,
When you spite me and laugh at my ways.
For then, yet again, the trigger is pulled,
And the same bullet shot to my heart.
For my pain isn't pain,
But an echo.
A pain, from you, I hide.'

Emma Carr (13)
Macmillan College, Middlesbrough

Football

A ball is flying in the air
While the referee is being fair
Then the magpies kick the ball
While Alan Shearer scores a goal

Black and white is the strip
Then Sunderland's player has a trip
He saves the goals, that's the goalie
But he moves very, very slowly

A streaker runs onto the pitch
Then he falls into a ditch
A ball is like the pitch's heart
Up and down like a dart

The fans, they shout, 'Hooray! Hooray!'
Overall they've had a good day.

Matthew Vaughan (12)
Marden Bridge Middle School, Whitley Bay

October Garden

Rustling leaves,
Bees buzzing.
Children laughing,
Chilled by the autumn breeze.

Did they notice that the nasty litter
Was spoiling the autumn garden?
Crisp packets and beer cans
Hidden amongst the leaves.

Sophie Horsborough (12)
Marden Bridge Middle School, Whitley Bay

My Cats, My Sisters And Me

Let's start with the cat,
The big, fat cat,
Who goes by the name of Binx,
Because he's a bit of a minx.

We will continue with the oldest,
Because she's the boldest.
An intelligent girl with a heart of gold,
Any man she sees, he is sold.

Next comes Domie
Who's slightly younger,
Bright and beautiful,
But always a wonder.

Then there is me,
A small garden pea,
Sweet and petite, but with a sting
Like a bee.

Last but not least,
The youngest of all,
Frankie the frightful,
Standing so tall.

Chelsea Howson (12)
Marden Bridge Middle School, Whitley Bay

The Sea

Boats stand still in the rough sea
Crabs pinch children's toes
A salty smell in the air
Shells clatter against the rocks
Fish swim through the seaweed
Slippy seaweed stuck to rocks
The sun sets behind the calm sea.

Danielle Fox (12)
Marden Bridge Middle School, Whitley Bay

Friendz

Loving hearts all around
Even when we're snug and sound

We stick together when we're free
We swap houses to go for tea

Everything we seem to share
What our friends tell us, we always care

We help each other when we're stuck
Even when there is no luck

On special days we'll go out
Have a good party, scream and shout

At the end of the week we all sleep at mine
We'll talk together, what we're doing in time

We'll always remember our friendship saying
Friendz forever stick together.

Georgia Whinfield (12)
Marden Bridge Middle School, Whitley Bay

Food

I like food, especially chocolate
It's nice and cold and very, very yummy
It goes inside my tummy

I like rice
It's very, very nice
I like it in the morning
When I'm very boring

But any food will
Make me smile.

Nicole Reid (12)
Marden Bridge Middle School, Whitley Bay

Seasons

Spring
Springtime, the plants are coming alive again
Springtime, the trees are fresh
Springtime, we run and shout under clear blue skies
The wheel starts to spin

Summer
Summertime is the brightest time all year round
Summertime heats all of the earth
Summertime lights up the world
The wheel is spinning

Autumn
Autumn time, leaves turning red, orange and yellow
Autumn time creaks cold
Autumn time, leaves swaying left and right
The wheel is spinning

Winter
Wintertime, the fog blinding all eyes
Wintertime, freezes time in motion
Wintertime, bones as brittle as branches
The wheel slows spinning and goes back to the start.

Tom Smith (12)
Marden Bridge Middle School, Whitley Bay

Sport

Football is cool
When you're playing for school
For rugby you need weight
But you can't hesitate
Basketball's fun
When you know you've won.

Callum Callighan (12)
Marden Bridge Middle School, Whitley Bay

My Family And Friends

My brothers are six and eight,
They like to play football and roller skate.
Their favourite music is rap,
They hate dance, especially tap.

My sister is only four,
She likes Sindy, Barbie and more.
Her favourite music is pop,
She hates R&B and hip hop.

My parents are really nice,
Mum likes cats and hates mice,
Dad likes water and hates beer,
My parents are quite queer.

My best friend's called Thamanna,
She hates being called Banana.
My other friend is Rubina,
She likes cats and hates bats.

Yasmin Begum (12)
Marden Bridge Middle School, Whitley Bay

Shadows

Shadows follow you everywhere,
Even when you are naked and bare,
They sometimes give you a nasty fright,
When you're sleeping in the night,
They creep past you in the day,
If you don't like them then you will pay.

Jessica Wragg (12)
Marden Bridge Middle School, Whitley Bay

The Mad Park

In I go,
Into this gloomy place,
The trees are weird,
They make a face.

The dogs are queer,
They look like they are mad,
I don't talk to them,
So they are sad.

The grass I'm standing on,
Is blue and hard,
I'm starting to sink,
It feels like lard.

Why is this place so ghostly?
Why is it so bare?
Why do I shake a lot,
When I am scared?

Laura Wilson (12)
Marden Bridge Middle School, Whitley Bay

October Garden

A rustling of leaves,
as the wind gently pushes them along.
Twigs snap under my feet,
and I hear the sound of bees going past my shoulders.
I feel the hard, wrinkly bark of the trees.
I see the conkers on the ground and the light, leathery roses,
the mushrooms hidden underneath the grass,
creatures getting ready to sleep
before the wild, winter breezes,
the swishing and swirling of the plants
as if they were on a dance floor.

Daniel Kingswood (12)
Marden Bridge Middle School, Whitley Bay

The Park

After school I pass the park,
Should I play,
Until dark?

Inside the gate, I sneak in,
A game of tig,
I should win.

Children laughing,
Having fun,
Playing in the afternoon sun.

Round and round,
The roundabout goes,
Where to?
No one knows.

I see the swing,
Birds start to sing.

High above, I soar,
To the clouds,
And back to the floor.

A baby cries,
I soon realise,
The sun is setting,
I'm forgetting,
I should be home!

Charlotte O'Neil (12)
Marden Bridge Middle School, Whitley Bay

Today

War, murder, guns, terrorism, that's the world today
Yes, no, on, off, that's the people today
Scrappy, clean, posh, dirty, that's the buildings today
What a place the world is with all this going on.

Daniel Crow (12)
Marden Bridge Middle School, Whitley Bay

Nothing

No hours without days,
No days without hours.
No darkness without light,
No light without darkness.
No life without death,
No death without life.
No joy without pain,
No pain without joy.
No past without present,
No present without past.
No future without time,
No time without future.
Nothing is nothing,
Nothing is nothing.
It never really ends,
It never really started.

Adam Sloan (12)
Marden Bridge Middle School, Whitley Bay

Holiday

Sun reflecting on the sea.
Waves splashing down on me.

Children are swimming in the pool.
Adults chilling, looking cool.

Adults sunbathing on the beach,
With the hotel in easy reach.

The reps are resting, having food,
While we are in a very good mood.

It's time to go, we're very sad.
We'll tell our friends the experience we had.

Anna Stevens (12)
Marden Bridge Middle School, Whitley Bay

Sport

Boots smacking the turf,
Shin pads protecting bones,
Strips shining brightly,
Ball hitting the back of the net,
Goal!

Gum shield hiding teeth,
Strips thick and sweaty,
Ball-shaped egg,
Boots with big studs,
Try!

The pads are thick,
But they have a big stick,
The game is tough,
But the people are rough,
The skates are sharp,
Goal!

Christopher Swan (12)
Marden Bridge Middle School, Whitley Bay

Your Team

The strips are always different colours.
The sticks have to be strong as can be.
The puck glides into the back of the net
Or to the keeper's pads.
The sweat will drip down your face.
All the padding will protect you from bone-crunching hits.
Your skates will guide you along.
Your skill will create a goal
For your team.

Craig Lydall (12)
Marden Bridge Middle School, Whitley Bay

Witch's Cat

I am a prowling witch's cat
My owner wears a pointy hat
I travel on her magic broom
As we zoom past the moon.

She has a huge mole on her nose
Which grows and grows and grows
She eats loads of pies which contain frogs' eyes
And no, I'm not telling you lies.

My owner's fat and hairy
She is actually quite scary
Her face is square
She has silvery-grey hair
I am a black witch's cat.

Marni Mather (12)
Marden Bridge Middle School, Whitley Bay

Technology, Technology

My TV plays like a baby
and gels with my PlayStation 2.

My internet hums like a bee
looking for something to do.

My computer runs like a dream
searching for its resolution.

My radio natters like my sister
trying to sort out confusion.

All of these things are so special
from a radio to a TV.

And all of the things are so special
because they all contain a part of me.

Thomas Flynn (12)
Marden Bridge Middle School, Whitley Bay

In The Morning

In the morning,
When I'm getting dressed,
I'm always thinking
Which clothes
Look the best.

My room is a tip,
My mum says,
'Less,
Of your lip!'

When I get to school,
I remember,
I forgot to revise for a test.

I still don't think
That this
Looks the best!

Amy Forbes (12)
Marden Bridge Middle School, Whitley Bay

Christmas

Christmas is for presents,
Holly on the door,
The snow is blanketing the ground.

Santa's coming in his sleigh,
'Ho, ho, ho,' he says,
Flying presents all around.

Christmas is a family time,
Friends gather round the tree,
All the presents found.

Laura Wall (12)
Marden Bridge Middle School, Whitley Bay

Your School

Windows and doors
Ceilings and floors
Tables and chairs
Too many stairs

A field and a yard
The teachers are hard
Boxes in stacks
Books on the racks

The head teacher's nasty
Dare eat a pasty
Cobwebs in corners
The teachers are moaners

Maths, English, art
The housepoint chart
Science, history, French
Go sit on a bench

IT, RE, PE
Run round, it's break, we're free
Technology, music, geography,
In English we write a biography

I would not go to your school
Because it's not very cool.

Marie Husthwaite (12)
Marden Bridge Middle School, Whitley Bay

The Ghost

A very small ghost from Calcutta
By day he hid in a roof gutter
At night he came out
To scream and shout
And leave his footprints in the butter.

Lauren Tudor (12)
Marden Bridge Middle School, Whitley Bay

Tiger

He lays in wait
For his next bait
A soft purr
From golden fur

His giant paws
With deadly claws
A playful bounce
A killing pounce

His long stripes
All different types
A hungry pack
Holding back

He sees his prey
He's waited all day
One great big leap
And two dead sheep

He lays in wait
For his next bait
A soft purr
From golden fur.

Phoebe Friggens (12)
Marden Bridge Middle School, Whitley Bay

The Night-Time

This is what the night is all about.
Shadows stretch here and there,
darkness closes in.
Stars twinkle in the darkness,
black cats curl up tight.
The moon shines bright high above,
moans heard throughout the night.
Nightmares are true, as cold as they come.

Gina Wade (12)
Marden Bridge Middle School, Whitley Bay

How The World Works

Mother nature blows the clouds.
Mother nature feeds the cows.
Mother nature can be cruel.
Mother nature has a rule.

The sea is quite a bit like me.
The sea trots and shines with glee.
The sea is often rough and ready.
The sea is sometimes calm and steady.

The morning brings the light to the world.
The morning leaves the dew behind.
The morning chases away the darkness.
The morning wakes up all mankind.

Mother nature can be cruel,
But so can we, that's why her rule is
She will evermore be there,
But not unless we show we care.

Matthew Wilson (12)
Marden Bridge Middle School, Whitley Bay

Perpetual Motion

Monday the sun comes out to play
Tuesday the wind swishes by
Wednesday the rain tears down
Thursday the heat stays awake
Friday the foggy mist comes today
Saturday the cold shivers away
Sunday there's nothing, it just waits till tomorrow
To start the week again.

Shiuli Rahman (12)
Marden Bridge Middle School, Whitley Bay

I Want To Be A Movie Star

I want to be a movie star
I know it sounds absurd
You may think it's not acceptable
Because of the rumours you've heard.

I want to be a movie star
That lifestyle looks luxurious
People say I'm bonkers
And that makes me so furious.

I'm going to be a movie star
No matter what it takes
I'll capture all the nation's hearts
And travel place to place

I'm going to be a movie star
Just you wait and see
When you turn your TV on
All you'll see is me!

Aimee Downey (12)
Marden Bridge Middle School, Whitley Bay

The Sea

The sea is a rough thug
But motionless like a sleeping lion
Always fighting with the rocks and the river
It's cold like a lolly
The sea is a nightclub
The fish are its visitors
The sharks are its bouncers
Then when man throws his net and spoils the fun
The sea wails and becomes the rough thug.

Mark Errington (12)
Marden Bridge Middle School, Whitley Bay

Seasons

When spring appears,
The summer nears.
The flowers grow,
The rivers flow.

The summer arrives,
The sun will rise.
Soon autumn will come,
The birds will eat their last crumb.

The autumn says, 'Hi!'
The winter is nearby.
The leaves will drop,
The plants will flop.

The winter is here,
Soon spring will appear.
This time is for joy,
To get a new toy.

Sam Erskine (12)
Marden Bridge Middle School, Whitley Bay

My Family

My mam is caring,
Loving and kind.

My brother is daring,
Truthful all the time?

My dad is sharing,
And has a good mind.

Take a piece from each,
And what do you find?

Me!

Emma Roberts (12)
Marden Bridge Middle School, Whitley Bay

My Journey Through Space

Moving swiftly through the never-ending dome we call space,
Not going too fast, this isn't a race.
Mercury, Venus and Jupiter shine,
It's almost as if all of it is mine.
Past the asteroid belt we go,
No one to tell us 'yes' or 'no'.
Saturn, Pluto, Neptune and Mars,
All of it, every single bit of it, is ours.

It's a long, dark, endless night,
All the stars are shining, burning bright.
The stars twinkle, everywhere we go,
Our knowledge expanding as well as revisiting everything we know.
It may be dark, but they are clear,
All the stars that have guided us here.
It never occurred to us just how big this could be,
This long-lasting maze where stars are free.
The planets keep us company, they talk, laugh, sing,
Their eyes are headlights, viewing everything.
But alas, our journey comes to an end,
And we have taken advice that the stars lend.
But before we reach Earth and the rocket base,
We wonder if we will ever return to this place.

Stephanie Legg (12)
Marden Bridge Middle School, Whitley Bay

Me!

My thoughts are a poem filling up my mind.
My mind is a book full of mysteries and riddles.
My book is a tale, exciting and magical.
My tale is my life, all about me.

Richard Newton (13)
Marden Bridge Middle School, Whitley Bay

Dark World

Moonlight is a silver sun
Keeping the night alight.
Moonlight is a silver force
Keeping the darkness under control.

Streetlights are giraffes
Carrying torches.
Streetlights are fallen stars
On the back of flying birds.

Night lights are dancing fireflies
Dancing all night long.
Night lights are green cats' eyes
Glowing until dawn.

Any light in the dark will do,
For we all need a light,
To help us through,
As this is a dark world.

Sam Tack (12)
Marden Bridge Middle School, Whitley Bay

School

School, school, what a horrible thought.
Teachers, detention, homework and rules.
Teachers, oh teachers, what do they tell us?
Nothing except nothing at all.
Rules, oh rules, what are they for?
You're not allowed to just walk out that door.
Time, oh time, where is it going?
Nowhere except nowhere at all.
At the end of the day what has school taught us?
Nothing except nothing at all.

Lawrence Rainbow (12)
Marden Bridge Middle School, Whitley Bay

When I Went Riding

When I went riding on Monday,
I saw a strong stallion coming my way.

When I went riding on Tuesday,
I saw a little foal, there he lay.

When I went riding on Wednesday,
I saw a magnificent mare in the field in May.

When I went riding on Thursday,
I saw a cart horse pulling some hay.

When I went riding on Friday,
I saw a young colt, in the field he did play.

When I went riding on Saturday,
I saw an Arab, its coat was bay.

But I couldn't go riding on Sunday.
A terrible storm, a terrible day.

Ruth Tonks (12)
Marden Bridge Middle School, Whitley Bay

Television

A picture that moves.
A tale in a box.
It's a brilliant invention, it really rocks.
It turns off and on,
And on and off.
You buy sweets or popcorn to nibble or scoff.
I really like it, I think it's great.
It's taken over my life.
It's my new best mate.

Liam McEwan (12)
Marden Bridge Middle School, Whitley Bay

Reflecting

When I went to school today, I thought of what I wanted to be.
Do I want to be a pilot, sailor or maybe a doctor, or how about
a dentist?
Then I thought, *well, how about a teacher?*

When English started we had to copy out the English rules.
When all the class had gone, and I was only left, my teacher said,
'It doesn't have to be perfect,
It doesn't have to be like the rest,
It doesn't have to be fantastic,
I just want you to do your best.'

20 years later, when I got the job I wanted,
I had an English class that was copying the English rules.
When all the children had gone and only one was left, I said to him,
'It doesn't have to be perfect,
It doesn't have to be like the rest,
It doesn't have to be fantastic,
I just want you to do your best.'

Taylor-Jay Hyde (12)
Marden Bridge Middle School, Whitley Bay

My Mind

In the morning, my mind is a factory starting up.
At school, my mind is an exploding bomb full of answers.
At lunchtime, my mind is a filter getting rid of pollution.
Back home, my mind is a rubbed-out blackboard.
Watching TV, my mind is an alert security camera.
Going to bed, my mind is a heartbeat slowing down.
Asleep, my mind is a light switch turned off.
My life is one big adventure.

Patrick Owers (12)
Marden Bridge Middle School, Whitley Bay

Dragon

The dragon stands tall and mythical
Waiting for someone killable.
When she sees them she will run
As fast as she can at them.
Dragons are killers,
Dragons are ugly,
Dragons will fly on wings so big.
Smoke coming out of her nose
After blowing a big fireball.
Dragons are fierce,
Dragons are fat,
Dragons are red and blue.
They may look cute but don't be fooled,
As she'll eat you up without a chew.
The dragon stands tall and mythical,
Waiting for someone killable.

Siobhan Kemp (12)
Marden Bridge Middle School, Whitley Bay

The Mysterious Mirror

Mirror, mirror, on the wall
Why do you stand proud and tall?
Why can't you move or laugh or sing?
Can you hear when the doorbell rings?
Do you feel sad or happy today?
Mirror, mirror, on the wall
Can you hear what I say?
Do you wish you could talk and play
Or do you like to be on the wall
Just watching my family in the hall?
Mirror, mirror, on the wall
What are you waiting for?

James Auchterlonie (12)
Marden Bridge Middle School, Whitley Bay

My Brother

My brother is a pain,
He drives me up the wall.
He grasses me up,
I don't like him at all.

He's small and quiet,
Just like a mouse.
He creeps silently,
Around our house.

He'll sneak up on me,
When I don't know.
And scare me to bits,
I just want him to go.

I'll kick him and hit him,
But then he'll tell.
Until I get punished,
And that's really hell.

He's my brother,
And I think he's dim.
Even though he's annoying,
I still love him.

Thomas Perry (12)
Marden Bridge Middle School, Whitley Bay

Chocolate

Chocolate comes in shapes and sizes
Inside wrappers I win the prizes.
Chocolate is my one true love
It's in my mind like a chocolate dove.
Flying around and flapping its wings
Chocolate is one of my favourite things.

Emma Dillon (12)
Marden Bridge Middle School, Whitley Bay

Dragon

Dragon hiding in a cave,
Guarding treasure night and day,
Killing off those strong and brave,
Come to slay him at his bay.

Dragon breathing smoke and fire,
Guarding treasure night and day,
If you see him it will be dire,
As it is or so they say.

Dragon tough, dragon strong,
Guarding treasure night and day,
Defeated only by siren's song,
Sleeping soundly he did lay.

Beth Newman (13)
Marden Bridge Middle School, Whitley Bay

War

The chink of armour
The scream of a warrior dying for honour
The warriors come marching in huge hordes
The clash and smash of silver swords

The clatter of hooves hitting the ground
At the end of the battle a king will be crowned
The thump of a body hitting the floor
Crows fly around and start to caw

The grass is covered in warriors' blood
A misfired arrow lands in the mud
The tip of the sword cuts into his chest
Finally his body has come to rest.

Josh Burrough (12)
Marden Bridge Middle School, Whitley Bay

Dragon-Half

I am a dragon-half.
I am half human, half dragon.
I have wings that make me fly,
All around the sky.
I have horns on my head,
They are stronger than lead.
I have a tail on my bum.
I am nothing but dumb.

I am a dragon-half.
I am half human, half dragon.
I have red eyes that let me
See super vision.
I have a nose that lets me
Have super smell.
I have two ears on my head
That let me hear super well.

I am a dragon-half.
I am half human, half dragon.

Mohiuddin Ahmed (12)
Marden Bridge Middle School, Whitley Bay

Shadows

Shadows are everywhere
They follow you up the stairs
Shadows are at your home
So you know you're not alone
Shadows are in the street
And watch when you eat and sleep
Shadows always follow you
Even when you never knew
My shadow always follows me
That's the way I want it to be.

Sarah Hakin (12)
Marden Bridge Middle School, Whitley Bay

Guess Who?

Pizza eater
Fanta drinker
Spider hater
Dragon lover
Stupid singer
Loud laugher
Scottish dancer
Rubbish reader
Wicked writer
Puppy player
Flexy flyer
Late comer
Heavy sleeper
Sweet shopper
Money waster
Bad sleeper
Pairs goer

I don't think you've guessed yet
But it's my sister, Jess.

Sarah Cummings (12)
Marden Bridge Middle School, Whitley Bay

What Is Happiness?

What is happiness?
Happiness is a smile,
Happiness makes laughs,
Happiness is a warm glow inside,
Happiness makes eyes twinkle,
Happiness is sunshine on a warm day,
Happiness makes smiles,
Happiness is getting presents at Christmas,
Happiness is going on holiday,
What is happiness? Happiness is simply a smile!

Nicola Glenwright (12)
Marden Bridge Middle School, Whitley Bay

My Dog Jackson

My dog Jackson, black and brown,
Waggling tail and a frightening frown,
His big white bone that he carries around,
Always making a crunching sound.

My dog Jackson, he's so cute,
His sharp, short tail and his shiny suit,
When I take him on a lead,
He goes off and runs full speed.

My dog Jackson can be rough,
Bites and scratches, he is quite tough,
Although he drives me round the bend,
He really is my very best friend.

Robyn Cadman (12)
Marden Bridge Middle School, Whitley Bay

What's For Dinner?

Cheese
Cheese, yellow, smelly,
Cheese, creamy, holes covering,
Cheese, getting eaten.

Mice
Mice, squeaking, scraping,
Mice, creaking, smelling, searching,
Mice, eating the cheese.

Snakes
Snakes, hissing, hiding,
Snakes, silent, creeping, sliding,
Snakes, pouncing, eating.

Adam Found (12)
Marden Bridge Middle School, Whitley Bay

My Dad

Taxi driver
Scuba diver
Great swimmer
Lousy singer

Ferret user
Fast chooser
Rabbit eater
Card cheater

Towel whipper
Knife flipper
TV liker
Good biker

Hard worker
Darkness lurker
Short waiter
Footie hater.

Stephen Charlton (12)
Marden Bridge Middle School, Whitley Bay

Star Pictures

Tiny dots of light
Shining and shimmering throughout the night
Always there, they're never gone
Making pictures big and long

Giant drawings in the sky
No one knows how or why
Connected with invisible lines from each bright dot
This is why they're never forgot.

Lauren Amis (12)
Marden Bridge Middle School, Whitley Bay

My Gerbil

Fight starter
Fast runner
Seed eater
Tail chaser
Total nutter
Finger biter
Nut cracker
Bar chewer
Water drinker
Face cleaner
Hard scratcher
Getting fatter
Hand licker
Biscuit eater
Short sleeper
Night crawler
Long jumper
Quick rambler
Cost a fiver.

Tom Charlton (13)
Marden Bridge Middle School, Whitley Bay

Ghosts

Ghosts are kind, but some are mean,
Some are smelly, but some are clean.
Some ghosts are friendly, but some are scary,
Some are bald, but some are hairy.
Some ghosts are happy, but some are sad,
Some are good, but some are bad.
I know one but he's my dad,
That makes me extremely sad.

Louis Wallace (12)
Marden Bridge Middle School, Whitley Bay

Sunset Sally

The fiery-orange sunset,
Is orange as a pet,
It is bigger than the moon,
And I'm sure I'll see it soon,
Have you seen it go up and down?
The birds are singing, a lovely sound.

The sunset sinks into the sea,
Have you seen it? Come and see,
Bubblebath is its smell,
You can't sell that,
No you can't.

The sunset has a great name,
As it's got a lot of fame,
It has a friend called Harry,
But her name is Sally,
Sunset Sally.

Sunset Sally brightly glows,
With all the colours flowing,
Along the edge it flames,
Every day is the same.

Rachel Butler (12)
Marden Bridge Middle School, Whitley Bay

The Shadow Horse

Out one night was the shadow horse,
Its mane and tail were thick and black,
It had dark, fine fur and had no flaws.
Its hooves noiselessly flew over the grass,
The stirrups shone silver through the darkness,
And the girl gracefully rode her shadow horse,
As into the night the two took flight.

Hayley Richardson (12)
Marden Bridge Middle School, Whitley Bay

Becks 7

Skilled player
Hard kicker
Good shooter
Pen taker
Goal scorer
Mint corner
Adidas wearer
Centre midfielder
Money spender
Posh lover
Rough tackler
Fast runner
Hair changer
Diamond buyer
Cool curler
Fair player
Hat-trick scorer
Cup winner
Crowd lover.

Laurél Davidson (12)
Marden Bridge Middle School, Whitley Bay

In Winter

When I open the door, I feel a windy breeze,
I look up at the trees and see no leaves.
The snow falls heavily on my head,
Now I wish I'd stayed in bed.
Christmas trees are all around me,
Turkey and decorations close in and surround me.
I slowly wake up, it was just a dream,
But it felt so real or so it seemed.
I look out the window, there is no snow,
It's the middle of July, still five months to go.

Bethany Ruddick (12)
Marden Bridge Middle School, Whitley Bay

The Sky's Sorrow

The miserable sky cried out its tears,
As the wind ran away, avoiding their fears,
The stray leaves were captured by a strong breeze,
Whilst trees' brittle fingers fell off down past their knees,
The gossiping clouds drifted away,
As the plants enjoyed this awful day.

The plants absorbed the teardrops in the soil,
As rubbish swam in old car oil,
A loose drainpipe started to shake,
And the lamp posts' heads started to ache,
Cats hissing under cars,
As rocks lay in puddles as if they were spars.

But now the plants have had too much,
And the soil is a watery mush,
The rubbish now sinks in an oily swamp,
And the cats are inside eating food with a chomp,
The flooded town drowns in sorrow,
But everything will be alright for tomorrow.

Clio Delcour-Min (12)
Marden Bridge Middle School, Whitley Bay

Kenning

Bad dancer
Rubbish singer
Monkey lover
Stupid laugher
Weird dresser
Good spender
Fishfinger eater
Coke drinker
Loud screamer.

Emmy Henderson-Todd (12)
Marden Bridge Middle School, Whitley Bay

Guess Who?

Rabbit lover
School hater
Indian eater
Coke drinker
Stupid singer
Shoe shopper
Good swimmer
Rubbish runner
Fast dancer
Loud shouter
Great sleeper
Annoying waker
Slow walker
Chatty talker
Lazy bather

. . . Stacey.

Rebecca Fairbairn (12)
Marden Bridge Middle School, Whitley Bay

The Strange City

The cars blink as people walk past.
The trees shake as people climb up.
The bins hop as people move.
The telephone shouts as people talk.
The pubs stagger as people walk in.
The taxi jumps as people get in.
The buses wave as people say hi.
The restaurants chuck food as people eat.
The slides open as children slide down.
The wind whistles as people go out.
The babies cry as adults scream.
The children play as the sun shines down.

Natasha Kaur Chhina-Beverley (12)
Marden Bridge Middle School, Whitley Bay

Guess Who?

Freckle hater
Football lover
Food waster
Headache maker
Time waster
Money spender
Great cheater
Bad sharer
Fast drinker
Tea drinker
Great joker
Bad climber
A short temper
Trouble maker
Loud shouter
Fast runner
Sister beater
Quick thinker
Bad swimmer
Long sleeper
Bad worker
Rubbish cooker
Girlfriend - never.

Karl Everiss (12)
Marden Bridge Middle School, Whitley Bay

October Garden

Crackling of leaves
Snapping of twigs
Buzzing of insects
Wind bashing my skin
Mushrooms hiding
Secretly hidden
Peeping out of the leaves.

Sam Patrick (12)
Marden Bridge Middle School, Whitley Bay

School

Chairs and tables
Drawers with labels
Desks with papers
Cutters and shapers.

Boxes in stacks
Books on the racks
Work on the wall
With displays and all.

Bags on the floor
Cobwebs on the door
The bin in the corner
The teacher is such a moaner.

And when it's homework day
The teacher will say,
'Sit down you little brats
Get out your work you silly rats.'

And if you say you forgot it
She'll say, '100 lines at break, now sit.'
The clock on the wall goes tick, tick, tick,
Now let's escape, quick, quick, quick.

Joe Feehan (12)
Marden Bridge Middle School, Whitley Bay

The Weather

The sun smiled
The rain raced
The wind wiggled
The snow shouted
The lightning lagged
The twister talked
The thunder tapped
The mist moored
The sleet skipped.

Julieann Moodie (12)
Marden Bridge Middle School, Whitley Bay

About Me

I'm an ant too small for the world.
I am a wolf in a pack.
I'm a cheetah, too fast to be patient.
I am a crocodile when I snap at my sister.
I am a shark when I shake in the water.
I am a hippo when I dance badly to hip hop.
I am a lazy lion when I listen to music.
I am a kangaroo when I do athletics.
I'm an owl out at night.
I'm a monkey, wild in the trees.

Anthony Blackwell (12)
Marden Bridge Middle School, Whitley Bay

The October Garden

Leaves moving gently,
Scrunchy, dry leaves,
Wind hitting my skin,
Brown, bronze and orange leaves,
Shaking and dancing,
Snapping and twisting,
Hidden secret mushrooms
Peeping out.

Emdad Islam (12)
Marden Bridge Middle School, Whitley Bay

October Garden

Blustering wind bashing my face
Snapping twigs underfoot
Hidden mushrooms
Hibernating underneath dry leaves
Just waiting to be squashed
The swaying and swirling of the trees,
Their bark, bruised and blistered.

Tasnim Ahmed (12)
Marden Bridge Middle School, Whitley Bay

My Doggy

Ball chaser
Tail shaker
Food eater
Basket sleeper
Water drinker
Bone chewer
Pie eater
Girlie liker
Good charmer
Food waster
Cat hater
Pillow eater.

Zoe Board (12)
Marden Bridge Middle School, Whitley Bay

Me (As Animals)

I am a pig when I eat a lot of food.
I am a dog when I bite people.
I am a penguin supporting my football team.
I am a pufferfish when I get angry.
I am a rabbit running with the ball.
I am a monkey climbing up the walls.
I am a giraffe when I run.
I am a hippo when I'm in the bath.
I am a lion pouncing on its prey.
I am a hamster doing somersaults.
I am a baboon meditating in the shower.

Craig Smith (12)
Marden Bridge Middle School, Whitley Bay

I Can't Think Of A Title

I can't write a poem,
It is so hard for me,
I really do try,
But it won't work for me.
I would write a masterpiece,
I would write a book or two,
I would write my heart out.
I would make people laugh,
I would make people cry.
I have tried all day,
I have tried all night,
But *still* I can't write great poetry.

Nicholas Armstrong (12)
Marden Bridge Middle School, Whitley Bay

My Mum

Pizza pincher
Penguin hater
Party pooper
Noisy singer
Nasty knitter
Stupid laugher
Long sleeper
Bad swimmer
Rotten singer
Chocolate lover
Cola drinker.

Antony Morgan (12)
Marden Bridge Middle School, Whitley Bay

Hallowe'en

Spooks and ghouls come out at night,
Beware, they want to scare you,
Ghosts will haunt and witches fly,
Beware they're out to get you.

Through the darkness,
Down the street,
Zombies stomp and stream,
You'd be safer at home, because,
They want to make you scream.

Run home now,
No looking back,
Just in case they're there,
If you don't run quick enough,
You're going to get a scare.

Laura Martin (13)
Marden Bridge Middle School, Whitley Bay

I Love Christmas

I love to sit up in my bed,
and think of presents in my head,
the decorations on my tree,
there's some chocolate Santas just for me.

I look outside and can clearly see,
there's some presents for you and me,
there's small ones, big ones,
eeny, weeny, teeny ones,
but the best thing of all is it's Christmas!

Natasha Johnson (12)
Marden Bridge Middle School, Whitley Bay

A Walk In Autumn

I went out to the woods in autumn,
I touched the rough bark on the trees,
I smelt the scent of rotten wood,
The leaves crunched as I walked through them,
It was as if there was a red and orange carpet laid out before me,
All the empty, wrinkly branches waving at passers-by,
I saw a hedgehog curled up in a ball, fast asleep,
I felt the light breeze brush my hair,
I saw the birds swooping for berries,
I heard the squirrels fighting for nuts,
The wood is like a relaxing moment of peace.

Amy Telford (12)
Marden Bridge Middle School, Whitley Bay

A Poem About Food

I like chocolate melting in a pan.
I like Diet Coke fizzing in a can.
I like beans, they make you pump.
I hate carrots, they come from the dump.
I would die for steak pie.
I love sprouts, that's a lie.
I love Sunday dinner settling in my tum.
Especially when it is cooked by my mum.
But best of all I like cheese.
It is the nicest with ease.

Daniel Cardwell (12)
Marden Bridge Middle School, Whitley Bay

Christmas Is Coming

Christmas must be drawing near,
because all that you can hear,
are people singing at your door,
decorations from ceiling to floor.

Snowmen are smiling in the backyard,
you've just received a Christmas card,
Santa Claus is on his way,
with lots of presents on his sleigh.

The Christmas tree is very tall,
tinsel hanging from the wall.
Have you wrote your Christmas list?
Watch for mistletoe, you might be kissed.

Jessica Steel (13)
Marden Bridge Middle School, Whitley Bay

Sweeties!

S ucculent strawberry laces to sing with.
W acky Wonka bars to waltz with.
E legant Everton mints to emphasise with.
E laborate eclairs to embroider with.
T riumphant truffles to trampoline with.
I mportant Imperials to impress with.
E xcellent Easter eggs to embrace with.
S taying all day with sweets to eat!

Ruby Downs (12)
Marden Bridge Middle School, Whitley Bay

My Family

My family, oh what can I say?
I'll try to describe a typical day,
My dad goes to work very early,
Then my brother gets up with a face that's so surly.

He dashes around saying, 'I'm still tired,
If I don't get to work, I'm sure to be fired.'
Mum says, 'You should go to bed sooner and save all this bother,
Then you might wake up happier like your younger brother.'

I feed all my pets, my hamster, cat and dog,
But my dog eats the cat food, he really is a hog.
Ours really is a happy home, that's all I can say,
I like being a member of my family each and every day.

Dale Dunnett (12)
Marden Bridge Middle School, Whitley Bay

October Garden

Swaying, swirling trees
Dancing in the wind.
The wind attacking my face
Snapping twigs
Buzzing bees
Bronze leaves crackling underfoot
Mushrooms camouflaged by dying leaves
Peeping out
As though they were spying on us.

Anna Bernadelli (12)
Marden Bridge Middle School, Whitley Bay

My Brother

Nose picker
Dog kicker
Room wrecker
Money stealer
Sweet eater
Bad runner
Orange drinker
Smelly farter
Stupid liar
Batman lover
Loud shouter
Bad jumper
TV watcher
Heavy sleeper
Sword swinger
Door kicker
Total nutter
Bad drawer
Seat diver
Worm keeper
Biscuit eater
Bike breaker
Drum banger
Money waster
Hair obsesser
Bad cooker
Rain hater
Sun lover
Computer buster
Fish murderer.

Chloe Webb (12)
Marden Bridge Middle School, Whitley Bay

Football

A football is hard
A football is round
A football is high
When you kick it off the ground

A footballer is skilled
A footballer is fast
When he gets injured
He may need a cast

A goal is wide
A goal is high
When you score
The keeper will sigh

A pitch is big
A pitch is green
A pitch is made
To make players' dreams

A ref is harsh
A ref wears black
He is there
To stop players hack

A manager is smart
A manager is devious
He has a laugh
But he is also serious

A coach is powerful
A coach is clever
A coach is paid
To make players better.

Daniel McClay (12)
Marden Bridge Middle School, Whitley Bay

The Afterlife

It is peaceful and quiet,
Gentle and calm,
Leaves drop,
Roses float onto your palm.

Surrounded by kindness,
Understanding and care,
People all around you,
It is unique and rare.

You'll never forget,
About your past,
All the people you loved,
Will always last.

As the breeze blows,
The grass sways,
Watching children,
Enjoying their days.

I travel on,
Filled with love,
So much beauty,
From above.

I wish I could have stayed,
The temptation was very great,
Hopefully with a full life,
I will return without a long wait.

I stretched and rolled over,
And woke with a yawn,
Realising where I had been,
Before the break of dawn.

Emily Flood (12)
Marden Bridge Middle School, Whitley Bay

It Shouldn't Happen

In the ring
Just before the fight
The adults bet
Who'll get it right.

Two battered dogs
Come face to face
Ready to brawl
In the adults case.

The adults start to cheer
Just before it starts
The dogs go to their owner
So they stay apart.

The fight has begun
They start to bite
But the owner's wrong
Making them fight.

The brawl is finished
There one dog lays
In the middle of the ring
With blood on his face.

The dog isn't moving
Or breathing at all
It is dead
Inside the arena wall.

Drew Moore (12)
Ormesby Comprehensive School, Middlesbrough

My Washing Machine

White, foamy, bubbly stuff,
Spilling out all over.
I've got a broken washing machine
And the bubbles are taking over.

It broke last week, last Saturday morning
And all my clothes had shrunk.
I called the electrician from next door,
Who was something of a hunk.

He fixed it though no doubt he did,
But it broke the very next day.
I tried to phone the company,
They said wait until next May.

It is only June now,
And my time is running out.
The bubbles have took over my house,
Well almost, just about.

So I've given up on what to do,
I think I'll just let go,
But wait a minute, what's the sound,
Oh wait, it's the . . . uh oh!

The washing machine has just blown up.
I don't know what to do!
Do you think that I should call someone?
I would if I knew who!

Sara Mawson (13)
Ormesby Comprehensive School, Middlesbrough

School Trip

A school trip away. Far away.
Say goodbye. See ya later.
Had my breakfast.
Ready to go. Blow a kiss
And say no more!

On my way, travelling along.
Excited now. Singing a song.
Ask the bus driver,
'How long have we left?'
He says, 'Not long, I'll do my best!'

Suddenly there - we all spill out,
Jumping for joy, we all shout.
Running along with my friends.
My teacher screams, 'Stop at the bend!'

And then I'm there, lying in my bed.
In an old scabby shed.
Wishing I was back home
In my real bed.
We're only at a scruffy place
Far away from my home.
Which is the best place!

Yolanda Hughes (13)
Ormesby Comprehensive School, Middlesbrough

Willing Washer

Don't put nothing in me,
If you do I'll make a mess,
You'll have to clean up for hours and hours,
To anyone it won't impress.

Turn me on and I'll kill you,
I swear I'm telling the truth,
I'll always muck up your clothes,
It's the truth from out of my mouth.

If you put stuff in me,
It will never come out again,
But really, really if you do,
I'll give you all the pain.

I'll make you clean the floors,
And all you dirty drawers,
You'll have to hand wash all the time,
'Cause I swear to God, you won't use mine.

I want to be for show,
But always feed me though,
You can use anything but me,
'Cause I don't like you, neither does she.

You're always wanting me,
But I don't want your need,
You always try to throw me out,
But you, you'll never succeed!

Samantha Collins (12)
Ormesby Comprehensive School, Middlesbrough

Why, Who, Is?

Why can't I smile?
Why do I have tears sliding down my face?
Why can't I go out and play to rejoice my heart?
Why is my face always blue?
Why am I not filled with happiness?
Why is my heart not rejoicing?
Why?
    Why?
        Why?

I wake up at night
And look in the sky at the stars.
And ask myself, why?
Why am I sad all the time?

Is there something bothering me?
Is it that my brain doesn't want me to rejoice?
Is it me, myself?
Who always wants my face to be blue?

Who will answer those questions?
Who will solve my problems?
Who will want me to rejoice?

Someone has a good answer for that?

Why, is and who?

Tafadzwa Kuwaza (13)
Ormesby Comprehensive School, Middlesbrough

The Pet Shop

There's cats in the corner
Meowing all day long
And there's untrained puppies
Letting off a pong.
In all those cages, there's the budgies
Going *tweet, tweet, tweet, tweet,*
Then in the box there's the tarantulas
With oh so many feet.
There's a big strong python
Uncurling itself slowly
And the hamsters in the cage
Doing a roly-poly.
There's some rabbits in the corner,
Who seemed to have doubled overnight,
Then there's the mice
Trying to escape with all their might.
It's hard work looking after all these
Cleaning and feeding them too,
If you end up buying one of these animals
I really pity you!

Kate Whitehead (12)
Ormesby Comprehensive School, Middlesbrough

My Dog

Why did we get a dog?
All it does it eat, poo and sleep
It scratches all the furniture
And rips up the curtains
Then it goes to sleep!

It wakes up starving
And runs about like mad,
It slops its dinner all over,
But it's my dog
And I wouldn't give it up for the world.

Michael Maloney (12)
Ormesby Comprehensive School, Middlesbrough

The Exploding Microwave

You plug me in the wall
And sometimes I just fall,
To be spiteful to you
You don't care when I need the loo,
No wonder there's a spillage
You just care about the fridge,
Or even just the oven
You show me no lovin'.

And on a night when you need me
When I'm bursting for a wee,
The oven and the fridge are no use
You've already eaten your chocolate mousse,
It's now your main meal
And I'm ready to peel,
I'm cracking up in my head
You might as well put me in the shed,
But oh no . . .
Bang!

Samantha Pryde (13)
Ormesby Comprehensive School, Middlesbrough

Washer Gremlin

I'm the monster in your washer
I don't go for anything posher
Your 'Boro tops are perfect to eat
Much better than lint and meat.

Your mum's new trousers
Mmmmmm . . . delish
Better than any rotten fish.

When your trainers go in a wash
They come out, they splish and splosh.

Your dirty socks taste like cheese
Once I ate a set of keys.

Aaron Boggett (13)
Ormesby Comprehensive School, Middlesbrough

Christmas Day

Christmas Day, hooray!
Jump up and down on the bed.
Fall off and nearly break my neck.
Open presents, filled with joy, ripping and tearing
Like someone's put a firework down my pants.

'Mum! Mum! Can we go down now?
I'm just bursting to open my other presents.'
'Yes, OK!'
Flying down the stairs like a rocket
Slap! Bang! Went straight into the door.

Ohhhh! Look at all the presents
And they are mine, all mine!
Opened them all in ten seconds flat.
Get dressed into my new clothes,
Cool it's dinner time!

After Christmas dinner,
Crackers, *bang!* Go bonkers,
Little bro starts to cry
Yuck! He's got a vomit thing going.

(They day has gone fast, don't you think so?)
Go upstairs, have a bath,
Go to bed
Nighty night!

Kelly Broad (12)
Ormesby Comprehensive School, Middlesbrough

A School Day

Get out of bed, sun comes up.
Can't stop yawning, grab a cup.
Boil the kettle, grab a tea bag.
Pour the water, read the mag.

Get your clothes, put them on.
Get your socks, put them on too.
Go into the room, grab your shoe.
They start to hurt, 'cause they're new.

Get to school, everyone's there.
People playing, girls doing hair.
Teachers come out, tell us to come in.
They all shot paper, into the bin.

Get in lesson, fall asleep.
Everyone shouting, except me.
Teachers talking, teenagers smoking.
Playing football, then teenagers choking.

Bell rings, time to go.
Rush home, watch my show.
Get in the bath, watch TV.
I shout, 'Goodnight'
They say it back to me.

James Blagg (12)
Ormesby Comprehensive School, Middlesbrough

Christmas Day

Christmas Day, rushing about,
People running, one big shout,
Heat is on, meat is cooking,
Lots of people opening and looking.

Clock strikes 12, dinner time,
Poured out a drink of lemon and lime.
Mam has to shout, dinner's done no doubt
People sitting and running about.

Eating dinner, drinking wine,
Eating meat, dog wants mine.
Finished dinner, onto pudding,
Finished mine before my cousin.

Feeling bloated, eating chocolate,
Wanted more but too late,
Went to bed, snuggled up,
Needed a drink, in my cup.

Tamsin Hugill (12)
Ormesby Comprehensive School, Middlesbrough

My Day

Waking up, wipe your eyes,
Alarm clock rings, time to rise.
Wash my face, get dressed,
Go to school, look my best.

Bell rings, lessons start,
Sit down, act smart.
Break time, in the sun,
Break ends, no fun.

End of school, home at last,
Watch telly, time goes fast.
Go upstairs, go to bed,
Go to sleep, to rest my head.

Lewis Harvey (13)
Ormesby Comprehensive School, Middlesbrough

I'm A Little Mouse

I'm a little mouse
too small for people to see
I run in from the garden
and past the widescreen TV.

I'm a little mouse
I'm going for my feast
until the woman spots me
and screams like I'm a beast.

I'm a little mouse
I see her with a broom
I think I better run
before I meet my doom.

I'm a little mouse
I'm going to my home
so now I'll go to sleep
for tomorrow I will roam.

Carl Thompson (12)
Ormesby Comprehensive School, Middlesbrough

The Needle

It moves closer to me
My hand is really shaking
As my teeth chatter
And my legs clatter
It's still coming nearer to me.

The big sharp point
Enters my hand
I'm ready to scream and shout
I feel no pain
It's time to go
Now I know what it's all about.

Shirley Halliday (12)
Ormesby Comprehensive School, Middlesbrough

Zoo Monkey

There is a zoo monkey,
Who likes to swing a lot,
He was a clever monkey,
He can say a lot of words.

He welcomes people to the zoo,
In a lively way,
He would sit down in the zoo
And sing all day.

He loves to get fed,
He loves to get watered,
Sometimes he goes crazy
And acts like a clown.

He sits on people's shoulders,
To get his photo taken,
He pulls a funny face,
Or jumps down on the floor.

As night-time draws nearer,
He begins to feel alone,
He walks in his cage
And sleeps till dawn.

Then the people flood in
And monkey awakes,
People they adore him,
He loves the attention he takes.

Liam Johnstone (12)
Ormesby Comprehensive School, Middlesbrough

My Horrible Hoover

I'm scared of my Hoover,
Of the noises it makes,
On the night when we are in bed
I think it's still awake.

Last Christmas Eve,
My mum cleaned the whole house,
There was not a spot on the floor,
Not even a mouse.

Santa Claus came,
With this big rucksack,
The Hoover was waiting,
It was ready to attack.

When we came down,
Santa was on the floor,
The Hoover was stood there,
It wanted more.

He started sucking up my mum,
I knew it was a mug,
I ran to the socket
And unplugged the plug.

We threw him in the bin,
He still had his glare,
I don't know why Santa Claus
Never came this year.

Dean Harper (13)
Ormesby Comprehensive School, Middlesbrough

The Arcade

As the door opened, I stood there all excited
My favourite atmosphere of fun.
The sound of car engines, slot machines
And amazing new games.

I walked towards the car racing machines
As I heard that engine noise
And people turning the steering wheel and gears
With more and more fun.

A kid ran by me, trying to get to the ski machines
Excited by joy and happiness,
A man stamped on the pedal next to me, trying to win,
With a buzz as the machine ran out of money.

And there I sat with my hands on the wheel.
They were racing me, pushing and ramming my car.
I'm angry, trying to win, wanting the prize.
On the verge, ready to scream!

Christopher Rose (12)
Ormesby Comprehensive School, Middlesbrough

Christmas Day

I wake up at the crack of dawn
About 7-8am, sometimes 9
Open my presents
Rubbish all over the floor
My mum and dad open the door
After I opened them we had a feast
Fit for a king
Then I hear the Christmas bell ring
Santa came down the chimney
For Christmas Day
Which is today
Hooray!

Christopher Metcalfe (12)
Ormesby Comprehensive School, Middlesbrough

A Day At The Fair

City wakes up, sun comes out
Have some cereal, smash the cup
Workers are awake, children crying
Tea or milk, people are flying.

Say good morning, say goodbye
People go to work, listening to babies cry
Where is the bus? I am in a rush
Here is comes, with a lot of fuss.

Grab a seat, on the bus
People standing, one with a huge fuss
I've lost the bus ticket, it's here somewhere

Conductor comes, gives me a glare
I will get off when I see the fair
Because I know I'll have fun there.

Jamie Williams (12)
Ormesby Comprehensive School, Middlesbrough

Bullies No More!

Jenny Johnson, a quiet girl
No more does she speak.
No more does she twirl.
The dancer, the princess,
The dancer no more.

Jenny Johnson, a quiet girl
No more laughter,
No more pearl,
The loud mouth, the chatterbox
The loud mouth no more.

Jenny Johnson, a quiet girl
No more Jenny,
No more girl,
The quietness has gone
And so has my pearl.

Nicki Adams (12)
Ormesby Comprehensive School, Middlesbrough

Sun, Sun, Sun

I am laying on the beach, getting a suntan,
Then out of the corner of my eye I see a big fat man.
'Look at that sunburn on him!' I said.

I am on holiday! Holiday!
The best time of year to play.
I am feeling happy! Happy!
I just wish we could always stay.

My dad is running down the sand
With my lovely mum heading for the sea,
He never ever seems to ask me.

I just let them get on with it,
It doesn't bother me, I would rather get my friends,
If I wanted to go to the sea.

The sun starts dying down,
But it is still very hot, we all go to the hotel
And start to pack our bags
Because tomorrow is the worst day of all,
We're heading back to Cornwall.

Ashleigh Blake (13)
Ormesby Comprehensive School, Middlesbrough

My Crazy Dog

My gigantic dog
has a tendency to lick
the face off our visitors
and cover them in spit.
As they wipe their faces
he jumps up for more
and as we are trying to pull him off
the visitors race for the door.
His tail is wagging frantically
so hard it knocks you out
when you hit the floor
he scratches you with his paw.

Matthew Carter (12)
Ormesby Comprehensive School, Middlesbrough

Soggy Peas And Greasy Chips

At the end of lesson four
The bell rang spot on 12.30
'Oh no!' I cried putting my pen down on the desk,
Don't want to go to have my lunch.
As I walked down the corridor,
I reached the dinner hall and sat down on my chair.
Then in a flash I leapt back up
As fast as a leopard could run
It gave me such a fright,
Soggy peas and greasy chips
It really looked a sight
I can't eat this,
This mushy mess.
This shouldn't be allowed
I'm gonna have to hold my breath
And gulp it down in one.
1, 2, 3, eh! it's so disgusting
I'm never trying it again.

Lisa Baker (12)
Ormesby Comprehensive School, Middlesbrough

Barbecue Days

The fumes of the barbecue all around
The sound of sizzling burgers
People rush for some food.

Everyone eats, now time for a sing
No one cares because it's a laugh.

As the day ends, people leave,
The night draws in
Around the trees.

Now it was time for my bed
I brush my teeth
And rest my head.

Robert Keenan (12)
Ormesby Comprehensive School, Middlesbrough

The Faulty TV

I am a faulty TV, I won't let anyone watch anything,
I only watch what I want to watch,
I always turn myself on and off.

I turn my volume up to full blast at night so nobody gets to sleep,
I turn to mute when everyone's awake,
So nobody can listen,
I only do this when their favourite programme is on.

When they turn me on I turn back off,
When they turn me off I turn back on,
On the nights I talk to everyone to keep them awake,
They never answer back so I talk even louder.

If they watch a video I will turn it off,
If they turn it back on I will pause the video,
They never get to watch all of the video,
If they put it on I will fast forward the video
So they hardly ever watch videos.

Philip Wilson (12)
Ormesby Comprehensive School, Middlesbrough

Nightmare Mobile

I'm a nightmare mobile,
Lurking in your bag,
So you can't press my delicate parts
I'm tucked away in the depths of your bag.
Come on, make a call,
Don't let's hang about,
I'll try my very best to ensure
That call don't make it out
And when I'm ringing furiously
As you scramble to find me
Out I come, stop I go,
So there you go, that is me
Now you know no one can handle me.

Andrew McGarva (12)
Ormesby Comprehensive School, Middlesbrough

Boring

Are we ever going to catch a fish?
Or just sit here and sigh.
When Mum asks what we did
I promise I won't lie.

I'll say it was the most boring thing I've ever done
All we did was sit and wait.
The line was dead and slack
No fish at all were going to take the bait.

We had our dinner at 12 o'clock
Had tea at six
I never thought there was any fish in this giant lake
Oh no, the line has snapped, it will take him hours to fix.

We tied a hook to the line
And threw it straight back in.
Finally the line ran wild
We held on to it, it was only a tin!

The first catch of the day - a tin!
This is getting very tiresome.
My grandad said I should go to bed
Only so he could sneak a bottle of rum.

I just get settled and heard a big yell
It's Grandad screaming for help.
He was struggling with the rod, it looks quite big
I run over to help with the struggle.

I pull my hardest, my face starts to flare
All of a sudden the rod flies in the air.

On the end of the rod there's a huge fish
That is the biggest fish I have ever seen.
The fish struggled violently, it looks quite mean
This is a day I will never forget,
Spending time with my grandad is totally the best!

Danny Wootton (12)
Ormesby Comprehensive School, Middlesbrough

Typical School Day!

Wake up in the morning
Have my breakfast
But still yawning

Hurry upstairs to get dressed
Brush my teeth in a rush
Pack my bags, what a fuss!

Get in the car
Zoom to school
Have a good day
And be cool.

Today is school photos
My hair is a mess
That was clever
I forgot my brush!

The flash comes
I can't smile
Come on Katie
Straighten your tie.

Lesson four and it's been and gone
I'm dreading the results
It's all going wrong.

Five minutes left before home time
Let's enjoy it and have a good time
It's finally last lesson and make it worth your while.

Katie Jacobs (12)
Ormesby Comprehensive School, Middlesbrough

My Best Day

Sun comes up, I'm awake
No one else up, swift as a snake
Go downstairs, get my clothes
Put them on without a fuss.

Into the kitchen, wake my dog
Open my curtains, there's the smog
Fill the kettle, put it on
Mum's up now, still half asleep.

Make some toast, love the smell
Dad's up now, there's his alarm bell
Grab a plate, go sit down
Watch some telly, falling asleep.

Half asleep, here's my dog
Wakes me up, my eyes in fog
Look at the clock, quarter to nine,
'Mum I'm late, gimme a lift!'

'Come on then, hurry up.'
'Watch out Daz, mind my cup!'
'Never mind that, you're late for school.'
'Do I have to go?' 'Yes ya do!'

Get there quick, paper on the door
I get out the car, huh! slippy floor
Ha, ha Mam - guess what it says?
School is closed, will be for days!

Darrell Finley (12)
Ormesby Comprehensive School, Middlesbrough

Left Out

My friend said she'd go to Club M with us,
But she's got new friends now.
She says she gets left out with us,
I don't know what she's on about.
We fill her in on all the secrets
And everything we say.
'Why can't we go back to the old days?'
'I'm with my new friends,' she says.
I don't know what I'm feeling,
I don't even know if it's real.

I don't need her anymore
I'm not even sore.
Me and that's who'll they'll be,
She'll know I don't need her anymore.
When she finally sees
When she's in trouble, she'll come running to me.
But what I say will please me most,
'I'm playing with my friends you see'.
We don't play together anymore,
Because we like the friends we have
So this arrangement didn't turn out bad.

Ashleigh Melton (12)
Ormesby Comprehensive School, Middlesbrough

The Puppy

I got a new dog today,
It was really cool,
It ripped my dad's slippers,
From years ago.
　　He likes to play,
With a ball,
Whilst he gets under my mum's feet,
Because he's not that tall.
　　We went onto a field,
He got quite scared of all the other dogs,
So he ran away,
But slipped and became a muddy puddle.
　　We took him home
And put him in the bath,
When we pulled him out,
He was white again, but the bath was brown.
　　But now that it's nine o'clock,
It's time for bed,
Even my dog has fallen into a deep sleep,
After playing with everyone.

Adam Blowers (12)
Ormesby Comprehensive School, Middlesbrough

Mean Machine

Flicker, flicker, the telly goes off
Flicker, flicker, the telly goes on
Flicker, flicker, the aerial goes wrong
The telly goes *kabong!*
I'm not just a telly
I'm a great machine
And if you don't understand me
I can really be mean
When you're watching your favourite film
I'll flicker and flicker
Before I switch off
You'll go mad and hit me
Then I will turn back on
And as you sit back down
And pick up your cup of tea
I'll flicker, flicker all over again
Right that is it, you're gone for good.

Paul Readman (12)
Ormesby Comprehensive School, Middlesbrough

Nature

The mountain
The mountain stands peacefully
When the wind blows strong
The peak is curved with snow.

The blue river
The blue river flows calmly
Over the boulders
Fish swimming between the rocks.

The roaring fire
The flames are orange and gold
The night is so cold
The warm flames heat up the night.

Phillip McGill (11)
St Edmund Campion RC School, Gateshead

Pets

The pigeon is quite loveable
Flying here and there.
Up and up they go
Soaring in the air.

The cat is a cuddly pet
That will chase after a mouse.
A very cute creature
To keep in your house.

The rabbit is great
Running around in the hut.
Occupying itself
Whilst the door is kept shut.

The last of them, but not least
The dog is the best of all.
It will run around all day
Going to fetch a ball!

Lucy Harding (11)
St Edmund Campion RC School, Gateshead

My Cat

I have a cat
Named Jake
And such a mess
Does he make!
He likes to bring
Home presents and things,
But why do they always
Involve things with wings?
But I suppose I have
To put up with that
Because after all
He is my cat!

Danielle Highton (11)
St Edmund Campion RC School, Gateshead

The Months' Seasons And Colours

Spring
Red and pink
Purple and blue
Spring is here
And it flowers too.

The leaves are growing
In the trees
Grass grows quick
Up to my knees.

Lambs are in the fields
Soft, fluffy and white
It cheers my heart
And I thought what a sight!

Summer
Red and orange
Pink and blue
Summer is here
To cheer up you.

All the kids are playing
On the green
Eating lollipops
And ice cream.

Autumn
Red and orange
Rust and brown
The wind is blowing leaves
Down to the ground.

Autumn is here
The trees are bare
The wind is blowing
No time to spare.

Winter
Grey and white
Black and blue
Santa Claus is here
To check on you.

To see if you're
In bed early enough
Because if you're not
He will cross off stuff.

Winter is here
The time has come
To eat your Christmas dinner
And fill your tum.

Sean Jackson (11)
St Edmund Campion RC School, Gateshead

The Dog In My Street

The dog in my street,
Loves to eat meat and lie on his mat all day.
He has white, fluffy fur, a patch on one eye
And laps up his water in seconds.

The dog in my street,
Is very sweet and loves to be cuddled.
He loves playing with cats and especially rats
When they run around chasing their tails.

The dog in my street,
Is not very neat when coming in from splashing in puddles.
He lies licking his paws and opening his jaws
Before going to dream about food.

The dog in my street,
Has a best friend called Pete
Who likes dreaming and chewing on bones.
They run and play fight in the dead of the night
And may never come home until dawn.

This is the dog in my street!

Joanna Harding (12)
St Edmund Campion RC School, Gateshead

Life In Poor Africa

Cracked lips, parched land.
Dusty promises of help at hand.
Hungry children on picture cards.
Won't help a land that's growing too fast.

I wish it would rain on Africa.
Wash out the pain of Africa
But rain won't bring help to the land
Just floods and tears and no help at hand.
I wish it would rain on Africa.
Wash out the pain of Africa.

Guns and bombs, tears and mud.
Luxury limos race through the blood
Children and adults walk miles every day
And they hardly ever get paid.

I wish it would rain on Africa.
Wash out the pain of Africa.
I hope something helps this country very soon.
I wish every day while staring at the moon.

Rachael Harding (11)
St Edmund Campion RC School, Gateshead

Bullies

Bullies can be big, bullies can be bad
But they definitely make all the other kids sad.
Bullies can be evil, bullies are cowards
They bash little kids when alone in the showers.
So victims out there tell an adult today,
Cos if you stay silent they won't go away.
I've got one thing to say to all of you bullies
Bullying's not a joke and certainly not funny
So next time you threaten a kid with a knife
Just think in your head he could take his own life.

Now could you live with this in your head?
Through your evil ways there's another kid dead.

Lee Gibson (11)
St Edmund Campion RC School, Gateshead

Going Down The Long, Dark Street

Going down the long, dark streets
Lighting up the street lamps.
As I ignite the lights
The streets will get some light
So you can see as you go
Down the long, dark streets.

Coming to midnight, getting dark
Best hurry up before supper.
Left a few out, ran back for supper,
Getting tired, shouldn't take too long.

Back out in the streets where it's cold,
Lighting up the rest of the lights.
A couple more to go, it's getting colder.

Now I'm finished I can go home,
Warm up in front of the fire.
Before I go to be . . . Zzzzzzz.

Kenneth Henderson (12)
St Edmund Campion RC School, Gateshead

The Funny Man

There was a funny man on telly
He liked telling jokes and rumbles his belly
He loved children and liked playing games
His imaginary friend is called James.

He made children laugh around the world
Some countries hot, some countries cold
Children think he's fun
With his funny face and sticky out bum.

All the children laughed at his singing
For all the joy he was bringing.
All the children loved his tricks
He balanced balls on wooden sticks.

Dean Birkbeck (11)
St Edmund Campion RC School, Gateshead

Seasons

Nature is a clever thing,
Everything is in sequence,
Summer, autumn, winter and spring,
How does it know what season we're in?

How do we know that it is spring?
New buds appear,
And birds start to sing
And everything is cheerier and brighter.

How do we know that it is summer?
Blue skies and the sun shines,
The weather is warmer,
Summer is my favourite time of year.

Autumn is season best,
The leaves start falling and the trees are bare,
And stand out from the rest,
I like to kick the leaves and stamp on them.

Winter has come once again,
The nights draw in
And Christmas has come and will remain,
Now it's time to start all over again.

Cassandra Cameron (11)
St Edmund Campion RC School, Gateshead

Animals

The mouse, shy and sneaky
The rhino, nice and meaty
A lion who will eat both.

A cheetah, fast moving
A snake, sly and cunning
A giraffe, sleek but long.

A monkey, small but smart
A hamster, timid and short
A hawk, loyal and swift.

Callum Whinham (11)
St Edmund Campion RC School, Gateshead

Imagine A Place

Imagine a place
Which is full of grace
Where the rabbits are free
Where I can be me
The squirrels run and pick nuts
There's no time for ifs or buts.

Imagine a place
Which is full of grace
Where the sky is full of blue
And it's waiting for you
The grass is bright
What a sight
At this beautiful imaginary place.

Imagine a place
Which is full of grace
The sun shines bright and so high in the sky
And the trees are old and knarled, my oh my!
The early sparrow feeds his chicks, with the worm from the ground
They squeak and gurgle but unlike the mother can't sing very loud.

Imagine a place
Which is full of grace
Where the wind seems to sing
And I sit on the grass with the picnic I bring
I crunch at the food and slurp at the juice
I'm so relaxed, I feel so free and loose.

Imagine a place
Which is full of grace
But now it's time to wake
And leave my dreams behind
Maybe I'll dream again at school again
But tonight I'll know what I'll find.

Antonia Armstrong (11)
St Edmund Campion RC School, Gateshead

RIP

The lightning crackled, the thunder roared,
The air was rough and wild,
The rain lashed off the path,
The weather was anything but mild.

        Dark shadows hung over the television,
        The rotten wood door opened wide,
        A croaky voice spoke out of nowhere,
        'Move them feet and come inside.'

I looked out of the patio doors,
I saw a gravestone,
I slowly walked forward,
But tripped over a bone.

        I blinked again,
        Couldn't make out what was there,
        I knew I really had to go,
        But couldn't do anything but stare.

My blood turned cold,
I was paralysed in fright,
A shiver ran down my spine,
It was such a dreadful sight.

        I stepped onto the grass,
        A skeleton was in my face,
        Engraved on the stone was RIP,
        I shouldn't be in this kind of case.

I screamed and ran in a flash,
Something scary happened tonight,
Nobody will believe me, they'll say it's just a dream,
I didn't believe in scary things until what happened tonight.

Ashley Puntin (11)
St Edmund Campion RC School, Gateshead

Our English Lesson

We had a great time in English today,
We laughed all of our troubles away,
We laughed and laughed away the class
And quickly the time did pass!

You see it started with Billy and Bob,
They had to snigger at Mrs Throb,
She did not know it was them, so she shouted at Jane,
While Michael threw a rubber at Kane.

The rubber bounced off Kane's head
And it hit the bully at the front, scary Ned,
Now Ned was not very happy,
So he turned around and spat at Nancy Pappy.

Nancy started to cry so her boyfriend Ted,
Chucked a ruler at Ned,
It missed Ned, it skimmed his ear,
It went flying and hit Elle's rear.

Elle threw a paper aeroplane,
It went whooshing and hit Danielle Blane,
She flicked her pencil rather quick,
It landed in Boris' mouth (after this he was sick).

Yes we had a great time in English today,
We laughed all of our troubles away,
We can't laugh now though,
She hasn't given our house heads a mention,
No, Mrs Throb gave us *detention!*

Emma Conwell (12)
St Edmund Campion RC School, Gateshead

Moonlight Shine

In the moonlight when it's dark,
all the dogs begin to bark,
don't you think this very queer?
Is it a sign that danger's near?

Path of silver, trees do shine,
now I know the night is mine,
do you think the silver's nice?
It looks like frost but not like ice.

I sit by the window and think aloud,
a silver moon often covered by cloud,
if only one could see such grace
and see the cobwebs spun of lace.

I go outside to the crystal night,
as the bats fly into sight,
but if you stop and think a while,
the silver runs more than four mile.

So next time when you see the moon,
think about the silver gloom,
think about the silver shine,
and the silk that looks so fine.

Rhoda Chambers (11)
St Edmund Campion RC School, Gateshead

The Weather

The raindrops, they feel so cold on my skin
But I'm by fireside, inside with my kin.
The sea waves treacherous to the sailor's eye
It was so scary it made me cry.

The wind, it blows nearly making me fall
A mouth so big it will consume us all.
The trees shaking like a frightened child
Then it calms, tender and mild.

The thunder, it roars like a caged lion
As scary as when someone's dying.
The lightning strikes when you think it won't
When you follow it I beg you don't.

The sun, it's nice and it feels so warm
It comes to you in a swarm.
The beach is the nicest place to be
We'll both go there just you and me.

This would all make a storm
Except the sun which feels so warm.
If you think it's bad it gets a lot worse
But this is the end of the verse.

Stephen Scott (11)
St Edmund Campion RC School, Gateshead

There Was A Little Man

There was a little man and he had a little gun,
Through the field, through the field he did run
With a big top hat and a pancake
Tied to his bum bum bum.

Running, running through the field,
Hunting, hunting for the bear,
In the wood, in the wood he did run
Searching for the bear, searching for the bear.

Finally found the bear, finally found the lair,
Sneaking up, sneaking up on the bear,
Hiding, hiding from the bear,
The bear wakes, he doesn't know,
He jumps, bear jumps,
They clash!
Slash, slash, bang, bang!

Adam Phillips (11)
St Edmund Campion RC School, Gateshead

Sisters

My sisters steal my stuff
and cover it in sticky fluff

They hide my stuff everywhere
on the dresser, on the table and under the chair

We push each other all around
upstairs, downstairs and on the concrete ground

We kick the punch and scream and *shout*
Dad wishes we'd sort ourselves out

Kind, noisy bunch we all are
even if we were miles apart

They're sometimes funny, sometimes smart
and I still love them in my heart.

Samantha Marley (11)
St Edmund Campion RC School, Gateshead

What Is Snow? What Is Heat?

Snow is a glacier fallen from the sky.
Snow is an adventure waiting to happen.
Snow is a magical dreamland so soft and cuddly.
Snow is a sparkling present fallen from Heaven.
Snow is a cheerful, cold and cloud-like ball
Which melts in your hand like chocolate in an oven.
Snow is happiness and joy with your friends.
Snow is preparing for unimaginable excitement.

Heat is a volcano erupting around you.
Heat is a sinister trick waiting around the corner.
Heat is like the pits of Hell, so outrageous, so evil.
Heat is like an unlucky parcel fallen from the sun.
Heat is an erupting blitz of fire which dehydrates
Like a man who has had no amount of water in thirty days.
Heat is preparing for the worst.
Which do you prefer?

Karl Burns (11)
St Edmund Campion RC School, Gateshead

The Countryside

When I think of the countryside
how green are the fields
and how fresh is the air
oh how I wish I was there.

A walk in the woods
a stroll by the river
oh how I wish it could last forever.

The peace and the quiet
the only sound is that of the birds
the sheep and the cows
oh how I wish for this peace.

Oh the countryside
how I wish I was there.

Michael Howard (11)
St Edmund Campion RC School, Gateshead

She's Not Like That

One of my pets is a cat,
A really strange cat that's really fat
The cat is greedy and likes to eat,
She likes to eat tuna and cat meat.

She's not allowed out so she squeaks all day,
Because she can't miaow but it would be annoying anyway.
She's her daddy's little girl and she's nicest for him,
But she wouldn't be as nice if she was thin.

We like her cute and we like her fat,
And we hope she stays just like that.
She might be cute and she might be fat,
But that doesn't make her perfect, she's not like that.

She might be cute but she likes to scratch the walls,
And runs away when one of her owners calls.
Her name is Pepper and she is a gorgeous cat,
I hope she stays just like that.

Emily Harrison (11)
St Edmund Campion RC School, Gateshead

Animals From Around The World

Cheetah cheetah you glow so bright,
Under beautiful stars at night.

Kangaroo, kangaroo, jumping around,
Making a most delicate sound.

Monkey, monkey, fooling around,
Strangely enough it never touches the ground.

Alligator, alligator, big snapping jaws,
He pounces and he pause.

Animals, animals, some big, some small
Animals, animals, some hop, some crawl.

Michael Gourley (11)
St Edmund Campion RC School, Gateshead

A Nasty Scare

When I went out for a walk one night,
I got a nasty, terrible fright,
Because someone shouted, 'Boo!'
I stuttered back, 'Who are you?'

And out from behind a lamp post,
Jumped out a scary, opaque ghost,
Then there was another sound,
That made my heart pound and pound.

Then there were footsteps behind me,
I heard a voice say, 'Look at me.'
I turned around and guess who I see?
It was a dressed-up person as a mummy.

Then they reminded me it was Hallowe'en,
Then they walked away as a queen,
So when Hallowe'en came the next year,
They were shaking from toes to hair.

Kirsty Parker (11)
St Edmund Campion RC School, Gateshead

The Man From Liverpool

There once was a man from Liverpool,
Who spent his life on a stool,
One fine day,
He fell in some hay
And hit his head off a tool.

His oldest brother was crazy,
His oldest sister was lazy,
The youngest sister is ten,
The other one is called Glen
And they all like the rapper Slim Shady.

Samantha Walton (11)
St Edmund Campion RC School, Gateshead

A Day

My eyes open.
I feel the fresh rays of a golden sun warming my face.
A new day, a fresh day.
Fresh.

I look out to the ocean.
The vast powerful waves are crashing to the shore.
White stallions racing through the waters.
Yet, how peaceful the sea can be,
Rippling, echoing,
Blue.

I smell the green earthy forest.
That secret soil smell,
Full of life.
Light floods through the trees,
Sending dancing patterns onto the earth bed.
Earth.

Dusk falls into black.
The silver moon floats, bobbing above the ocean.
I see darkness, pitch-black, stark, sheer beautiful black.
The stars light up the night sky
Like a million twinkling Christmas lights.
My beautiful world.

Frances Saint (11)
St Edmund Campion RC School, Gateshead

To Have A Friend

Do you have a friend

Who will be there till their end?

To take care of you

A friendship that's true

Some people have one, whereas I have two

Who are they? You've got to guess who

To have a friend who cares

Is to have a friend who dares

To have a friend is rare

So always be a pair

Who is yours? Old or new?

To have a friend, just like you!

Olivia McCann (13)
West Redcar School, Redcar

The Bully

The bully is big and bold
at times they can never be told.
They chase you around the school
of course they think it's cool.

They go down the line one by one
but don't worry, they will soon be gone.
They act clever in front of teachers
they go around hurting small, delicate creatures.

They hurt you really bad
which makes you really sad.
And as soon as you tell someone
it won't be long until they are long gone.

Emma O'Rourke (14)
West Redcar School, Redcar

Mamma

This rhyme is for someone special
Who makes my life worthwhile
I'm thinking of you Mamma
When you've a washing pile.

But still I'll do the things I do
To help you on your way
So Mamma don't you worry
I see you through your day.

So take this rhyme with pleasure
That I have wrote for thee
To say that all things measure
Just like they ought to be.

Mamma you enjoy every day
In each and every way
And Mamma don't you fear
I'll always be near.

Michael Delaney (13)
West Redcar School, Redcar

It's a Twin Thing

The gun's just gone
and I'm not number one.
Charlie's first again,
huh, he's such a pain.

I'm not hard enough,
and Charlie's too tough.
My brain's the biggest,
but he's the fittest.

We get on great,
he's even my mate,
but . . .
It's hard being a twin,
you've always got to win.

Stacy Young (13)
West Redcar School, Redcar

Descriptive Poetry About An Object
We Use Nearly Every Day

The lifeless stack lies there on the floor, waiting there so still,
so quiet, to capture its prey.

With its two snakes wrapping around your body,
clenching their tails to keep it secure.

Its mouth open when you are about to feed it metal,
paper, plastic, wood and rubber.

It can be worn lots and lots of different ways.

It can be light or heavy, it comes in all different shapes and sizes,
it comes in different colours, you'll be amazed how many.

When it is secured on your body, you can be sure it won't move.

The patterns on it are all different, one may be squares of colour
another may just be one colour.

When you go to school, it isn't always with you if you take one.

If you still haven't got any idea, here's an easy clue . . .
it holds your book.

Sarah Turner (13)
West Redcar School, Redcar

Beach

B eautiful beach on a nice sunny day
E verlasting sunshine, what else can be better?
A fter an ice cream and a stroll along the beach
C hasing closer to the sea, when will I reach?
H appy days are coming and going
    I knew that the beach was where I belonged.

Elizabeth Smith (14)
West Redcar School, Redcar

Sister

I love my sister to pieces,
I am her number 1 fan,
She gives me most of her clothes,
Which everyone seems to know.

It's fun to have a big sister,
That I get on so well with,
We look alike in different ways,
So our dad seems to say.

She buys me little gifts,
Which are always so thoughtful,
We're always telling stories,
Which can be quite awful.

I wouldn't change my sister,
For anything in the world,
We always have a laugh,
Whenever we really can.

I love my sister to pieces,
I am her number 1 fan!

Carly Leigh Nolan (13)
West Redcar School, Redcar

My Football Poem

F ootball boots scrape across the floor as you run towards
                                    the goal and the ref shouts
'O ffside,' so there is a free kick being taken by Giggs and
O h, it's a goal, it was a
T errific goal by
B eckham for United
A s he heads it in from Giggs' free kick.
L eeds United Football Club
L ose to Man United, that put them bottom of the league.

Nathan Scrafton (13)
West Redcar School, Redcar

The Graveyard

I wake with a fright, I don't want to go,
Fear's in my heart, I feel so low.
I get changed, my clothes are dull,
The tears well up, I feel so full.

I step outside, the air is so cold,
The flowers I bought start to unfold.
I want to go all alone,
I don't want them to hear me moan.

My saliva starts to dry,
The tears want to come out, I need to cry.
I lay my flowers down, they won't last for long,
In my head I sing his favourite song.

The atmosphere's silent,
The way he died was violent.
All my tears I have cried,
And he's only just died.

Kerry Melville (13)
West Redcar School, Redcar

Playground

I walked into the playground and got one huge stare,
The teachers, dinner ladies and headmaster, they were also aware,
My heart was beating faster than it ever had before,
Little did I know what was going to be in store,
Then the teacher approached me . . . and asked me what's my name,
I told her, 'Lucy, Miss,' and put my head down in shame,
The other kids were laughing for I was new into their class,
I put my hand in my pocket and found my dinner pass,
I didn't want to wait 'til dinner time, I wanted to go home now,
The teacher wouldn't let me pass, so now I don't know how!

Lucy Would (13)
West Redcar School, Redcar

What Am I?

I am helpful to you
I can come in packs of two
I smell so nice
Use me daily, that's good advice
Sometimes I sting
People use me and sing
I don't taste so good
People being clean could
I can make big bubbles
As your bathtime doubles
But you use me on a morning
But now I'm warning
Don't get me in your eyes
Because it's not very wise
Have you guessed yet?
I'm soap!

Jamie Lewis (13)
West Redcar School, Redcar

Sweets

Nice and sweet,
Rainbow colours,
We share them with friends,
It's like the bag never ends.

Toffees and chews,
Pineapple chunks and strawberry sherbets,
So many flavours,
So much to choose from,
What would we do if all the sweet shops were gone?

We all enjoy a bag of sweets,
Every now and again.

Sweets are the best,
Nothing like a school test!

Samantha Knight (13)
West Redcar School, Redcar

Graveyard

The tombstones grey and rotting away
The mud slowly sinks where they lay
The names of people, old and new
The spooky mist that covers you
The trees around are tall and thin
They surround you and swallow you in
The writing on them fades away
That's when you know they've gone far away
Never to see your face again
The fence around it, black and rusty
The doors to get in are very dusty
There's no way out
Except over the wall
Where the spikes stick out
The graveyard is a spooky place
Where people go and there remain.

Emma Readman (13)
West Redcar School, Redcar

My Best Friend

My best friend is the best ever
She can sing and dance, and she's still dead clever.
I see her every day at school,
My other friends think she's really cool.
She helps me with my work in class,
So in the test I'm sure I'll pass.
She keeps me doing right from wrong,
We've known each other three years, not long.
But still I know she's my best friend,
We'll go on until the very end.

Kirsty Bass (13)
West Redcar School, Redcar